Expanding the ...

The public promotion of diverse books through the We Need Diverse Books campaign has added to the awareness of the need to promote, teach, and research books by all types of diverse authors and about a wide range of diverse characters. With this book series, we will survey and discuss the history of African American authors of young adult literature.

We separate this history into three two-decade periods beginning in 1960. The first book covers the first of what we classify as three waves of African American young adult literature. In the 1960s and into the 1980s, the production of books by and about African Americans in the young adult classification was slim. The first book covers the first wave, which we consider the groundbreaking work of four pioneers: Virginia Hamilton, Walter Dean Myers, Mildred Taylor, and Julius Lester.

The second wave, covered in the second book of the series, consists of a group of authors who began writing in the late 1980s. This group consists of eight authors who expanded the foundation and built a crucial reputation that garnered a variety of nominations and awards. These authors are Rita Williams-Garcia, Jacqueline Woodson, Angela Johnson, Nikki Grimes, Sharon Draper, Christopher Paul Curtis, Sharon G. Flake, and Jewel Parker Rhodes. A few of these authors also write children's books, but their major contributions are in the area of middle grades or young adult literature. They are, without question, the major contributors during this time period. There are several other authors who have a large catalog of children's books who also have one or two young adult novels, but their reputation rests squarely in the category of children's literature.

Given the growth of young adult literature from the 1980s and through the early years of the twenty-first century, some would find it strange that only twelve authors, four in the first wave and eight in the second wave, are classified as writers of African American young adult literature. Yet, this is the case. Other authors also wrote books that would be considered young adult literature, but they were either not well received or not adequately promoted. There are others who have reputations as traditional adult authors whose works are actively read by adolescents, but they are not authors of young adult literature.

For example, Harlem Renaissance authors are often taught in schools, but they are hardly writers of young adult fiction. Others, for example, Ralph Ellison, Richard Wright, James Baldwin, Zora Neale Hurston, Lorraine Hansberry, Nikki Giovanni, Gwendolyn Brooks, and August Wilson, have a presence in middle school and high school curricula, and these authors are African American representatives in the traditional canon. More contemporary African American artists are also read by adolescents—Toni Morrison, Alice Walker, Rita Dove, and Walter Mosley—but again their target audience is much older.

The third book covers the third wave and paves the path into the twenty-first century. Without a doubt, there is an abundance of authors writing and establishing a literary reputation. From this time period, we highlight eight authors who began publishing in the twenty-first century and have garnered awards and significant literary reputations in a relatively short period of time. These authors are as follows: Andrea Davis Pinkney, Shelia P. Moses, Coe Booth, Kwame Alexander, Kekla Magoon, Varian Johnson, Renee Watson, and Jason Reynolds. There are others who deserve to be read and watched, but at this point in time, these authors have separated themselves from the rest. They are writing with more variety, in more genres, and with stronger voices.

African American Authors of Young Adult Literature
Edited by Steven T. Bickmore and Shanetia P. Clark

*On the Shoulders of Giants: Celebrating African American Authors of
Young Adult Literature* (2019)
*Expanding the Foundation: African American Authors of Young Adult
Literature, 1980–2000* (2022)

Expanding the Foundation

African American Authors of
Young Adult Literature, 1980–2000

Edited by
Steven T. Bickmore
Shanetia P. Clark

ROWMAN & LITTLEFIELD
Lanham • Boulder • New York • London

Published by Rowman & Littlefield
An imprint of The Rowman & Littlefield Publishing Group, Inc.
4501 Forbes Boulevard, Suite 200, Lanham, Maryland 20706
www.rowman.com

6 Tinworth Street, London, SE11 5AL, United Kingdom

British Library Cataloguing in Publication Information Available

Library of Congress Cataloging-in-Publication Data

Names: Bickmore, Steven T., editor. | Clark, Shanetia P., editor.
Title: Expanding the foundation : African American authors of young adult
  literature, 1980–2000 / edited by Steven T. Bickmore, Shanetia P. Clark.
Description: Lanham : Rowman & Littlefield, [2022] | Series: African
  American authors of young adult literature: a three volume series ; 2 |
  Summary: "This book surveys and discusses the history of African
  American authors of young adult literature"—Provided by publisher.
Identifiers: LCCN 2021032109 (print) | LCCN 2021032110 (ebook) | ISBN
  9781475843552 (cloth) | ISBN 9781475843569 (paperback) | ISBN
  9781475843576 (epub)
Subjects: LCSH: American literature—African American authors—History and
  criticism. | Young adult literature, American—History and criticism. |
  American literature—20th century—History and criticism. | LCGFT:
  Literary criticism.
Classification: LCC PS153.B53 E97 2022 (print) | LCC PS153.B53 (ebook) |
  DDC 810.9/928208996073—dc23/eng/20211005
LC record available at https://lccn.loc.gov/2021032109
LC ebook record available at https://lccn.loc.gov/2021032110

Contents

Foreword

Nancy D. Tolson

The beauty of the kaleidoscope changes constantly with each turn. Inside the tube are colorful pieces that together create a variety of intricate patterns. The most important action of the kaleidoscope is that it must be held up to a light source for the light to radiate through the transparent bottom that confines the many movable colorful pieces. Holding the kaleidoscope down without a light source only displays figures of gray moving around in a tube.

Oftentimes young adult literature by African American authors is looked at like the pieces in a kaleidoscope. Books that celebrate the African American experience are only shown during a light show that is controlled by publishers, teachers, or librarians. The books are pulled out during special occasions to emphasize the uniqueness of the African American experience instead of kept out on the daily. The stories are captured inside an elongated tube with a peephole that when turned shows beautiful configurations and colorful commonalities that can only be seen with one eye. The viewer is never able to see the full view.

The collection of essays in *Expanding the Foundation: African American Authors of Young Adult Literature, 1980–2000*, edited by Steven T. Bickmore and Shanetia P. Clark, will assist in dismantling this literary kaleidoscope. Each essay chips away at this tube that represents the unfamiliar pieces that teachers and librarians don't know how to use. It may be uncomfortable to discuss the literature because it is rarely out long enough for people to become familiar with it.

Bickmore and Clark crack open the kaleidoscope with chapters on eight African American authors of young adult literature. Their books are no longer relegated to confining spaces and only suggested for book reports or small book discussions. The eleven scholarly essays in this book detail the intricate patterns, specific colors, and highlights that sparkle outside the kaleidoscope to emphasize each author's book(s), and this makes me very happy.

Bickmore and Clark's essay collection spans a period of twenty years to cover books by authors that have been part of the literary foundation of young adult literature even though sometimes they have been confined to special appearances or collections. *Expanding the Foundation* brings new readers to the work of Jacqueline Woodson, Angela Johnson, Nikki Grimes, Sharon Draper, Christopher Paul Curtis, Sharon G. Flake, Rita Williams-Garcia, and Jewel Parker Rhodes. The chapters overview each author and provide an introduction for teachers who may not be familiar with the authors or their work. I have read and written on many of these authors, and in reading the essays in this collection I felt as if I was learning something new about an old friend.

The learning activities herein are marvelous tools that can nudge students to read historical fiction while understanding contextualized historical references. How ingenious to create an assignment to read the US Fugitive Slave Act of 1850 with purpose and insight to capture a stronger understanding of a story on slavery. I applaud activities that promote book discussions concerning the topic of social justice to tie in contemporary issues.

Encouraging students to master the habit of journaling as they read can be a lifelong treasure for students. Coupling this habit with the ability to express oneself through prose and poetry forms a new lens of social analysis. As I read, I saw the pieces inside the kaleidoscope begin to float outside the tube, and I am elated to know that these activities can give teachers *and* students the opportunity to truly soar.

Thank you, Steven T. Bickmore and Shanetia P. Clark, for this opportunity to read *Expanding the Foundation: African American Authors of Young Adult Literature, 1980–2000* and for allowing me to celebrate this collection through this foreword.

Nancy D. Tolson
University of South Carolina
African American Studies

Introduction

Steven T. Bickmore and Shanetia P. Clark

This book, like many books, has been too long in the making. Almost a year ago, in March 2019, we were ready to read through the submitted chapters and finish our own contributions to the book. Then we began to feel the trauma of COVID-19 as we moved to virtual education and dealt with family issues and illnesses of our own. To compound this, some of our contributors also found that a difficult reality had entered into their lives as well.

We are remarkably proud of the first volume in this series, *On the Shoulders of Giants: Celebrating African American Authors of Young Adult Literature* (2019), which features the works of the four dominant authors during the founding and struggling years, from 1960 to 1980, of young adult literature. In that book, we, along with our contributing chapter authors, make the case for Mildred Taylor, Virginia Hamilton, Julius Lester, and Walter Dean Myers as the authors who paved the way and carried the weight of representation.

We label this role as a representative standard-bearer as a burden that is both unfair and marginalizing. In part, we suggest that publishers did not look for more African American authors or, finding them, did not nurture or promote their development when they already had such talented authors on whom they could rely.

In that first book, Deborah Taylor provides a chapter that surveys the development of the Coretta Scott King Award, which clearly recognizes other talented authors, but the chapter emphasizes that in the early years many African American authors were focused on children's literature and not the emerging classification of young adult literature, which focused primarily on the realistic problem novels.

In reality, publishers were not trying to push the field beyond series fiction—Nancy Drew, the Hardy Boys, sentimental pulp fiction reminiscent of after-school television specials, or the variety of formula sports and romance fiction prevalent in postwar America. Indeed, conversations about diversity and inclusion in publishing lagged significantly behind the actions of voting rights advocacy or the civil rights movement that were occurring as young adult literature strived to establish itself as a legitimate genre. Yet, these four authors were remarkable talents who continued to write and supported the next wave of authors featured in this second volume. We wish it were true that the number of new African American authors quadrupled or even tripled between 1980 and 2000. In fact, after examining the awards, the number of books produced, and the authors who were held in high regard, the number only doubles from four to eight.

Within the field there was movement. There was more inclusion of African American authors; as Taylor, Hamilton, Lester, and Myers continued to write, others were included. The eight authors who emerged during this next wave are Jacqueline Woodson, Angela Johnson, Nikki Grimes, Sharon Flake, Sharon Draper, Christopher Paul Curtis, Rita Williams-Garcia, and Jewell Parker Rhodes—all of whom have made significant contributions to the field of young adult literature. Most continue to be quite prolific into this century, and their works are staples in school libraries.

The COVID-19 era slowed down the production of this book. Yet, current events reminded us that the book is timely. We continue to argue that there is a place for books highlighting the achievements of African American authors. The death of George Floyd and the resulting reckoning for racial justice prompted society to read and share more stories about the African American experience. These events coincided with the contentious 2020 presidential election followed by the "big lie" that the election was stolen.

For us, this confusion and intentional misdirection are inexcusable. Most towns and cities where allegations of stealing the election surfaced were voting districts with large concentrations of Black and Brown voters. This reaffirms Bishop's (1990) advice that children—all children—need windows, mirrors, and sliding glass doors. She also asserts that expanding the texts helps to confront and disrupt "dangerous ethnocentrism." Black and Brown children see plenty of books that function as a window into a world they do not always get to experience firsthand. It is time for teachers and librarians to discuss with White children books that provide windows into unfamiliar worlds and direct them to this reading. These stories can be not only informative but also build empathy and understanding.

We need more stories and more perspectives. The authors in this volume are evidence that the work of representing the African American experience continues. In many cases, our graduate students have highlighted injustices that many, if not all, of the members of this community have experienced and confronted. In the midst of these injustices, these authors still tap into moments of joy and laughter. By showcasing such lighthearted and familiar moments, the fullness of African American lives shines. It is unfair—as well as disingenuous—to only illuminate heavy stories.

We point directly to the landmark contributions of Curtis's *The Watsons Go to Birmingham—1963* (1995), Woodson's *Brown Girl Dreaming* (2014), and Draper's *Stella by Starlight* (2015) as examples of how these authors present stories of families—both their own and imagined—in all their fullness, including both joys and frustrations. These authors not only create works of high literary quality; they are also notable for their dignity and their frank and honest storytelling.

This volume has a chapter for each of these eight authors, focusing on their critical reception as authors and discussing in detail a single representative work. They also offer individual, small-group, and whole-class activities that will engage students in the works. These activities are presented with several goals in mind. First, they cover a variety of standards within the English language arts curriculum without drawing attention to them in an awkward or didactic manner. We trust that teachers, curriculum specialists, librarians, and English educators can determine the standards that apply. Second, the activities are fluid in that they can be used with any text. Instructors need not be limited to the text the chapter authors use as a model; activities may be easily adapted to any of the works of the authors presented in this volume. Indeed, instructors who practice and master these activities will find that they are a valuable set of tools to incorporate into a teacher's toolbox. Many of them can be carried out without additional technology in the classroom. Others require computers and other digital tools and offer teachers and students the opportunity to make a variety of cross-curricular connections.

While we explore the achievements of eight significant authors, the book does have eleven chapters. We were able to dig deeper into the work of three of our authors. While all the authors are deserving of more academic and instructional attention, we have chosen Jacqueline Woodson, Nikki Grimes, and Sharon Draper for deeper discussion. Here we skirt the focus of critical reception and concentrate on a discussion of a significant work and provide additional activities, paying special attention to what might be done before reading the text, what can be done during reading, and what can enhance student understanding upon completion of the text. Each of these "bonus" chapters follows the main chapter pertaining to that author to maintain flow and continuity. The additional chapter on Woodson focuses on her novel *From the Notebook of Melanin Sun* (1995) and discusses the themes of coming of age and sexual identity. An additional chapter on Grimes allowed the authors of chapter 4, Napoli and Ward, to address Grimes's remarkable memoir in verse, *Ordinary Hazards* (2019), and suggests ways to include personal writing in the classroom.

The second chapter on Draper examines *Stella by Starlight*, a narrative inspired by Draper's grandmother's experiences in a small Southern town. This narrative references the ominous presence of the KKK as well as African American participation in the Olympic Games. Several activities ask students to explore how a variety of diverse populations have participated in Olympic events throughout the years.

Considering that all the authors featured in this book are alive at the date of publication, we look forward to many more contributions from them in the future. They represent important and powerful voices in the history of young adult literature in general and examples of the expanding voices of African American authors. We encourage you to ensure that your favorite schools and teachers have both this volume and the first volume in this series as an essential part of their collections.

REFERENCES

Bickmore, S. T., & Clark, S. P. (2019). *On the shoulders of giants: Celebrating African American authors of young adult literature*. Lanham, MD: Rowman & Littlefield.

Bishop, R. S. (1990). Mirrors, windows, and sliding glass doors. *Perspectives: Choosing and Using Books for the Classroom*, 6(3).

Curtis, C. P. (1995). *The Watsons go to Birmingham—1963*. New York: Delacorte.

Draper, S. M. (2015). *Stella by starlight*. New York: Atheneum Books for Young Readers.

Grimes, N. (2019). *Ordinary hazards: A memoir*. Honesdale, PA: Wordsong.

Woodson, J. (1995). *From the notebooks of Melanin Sun*. New York: Blue Sky Press.

Woodson, J. (2014). *Brown girl dreaming*. New York: Nancy Paulsen Books.

Chapter 1

"We're All Just People Here"

Freedom, Hope, and Migration in Brown Girl Dreaming

KaaVonia Hinton

In 1992, Dr. Rudine Sims Bishop described Jacqueline Woodson as one of the "most prominent African American literary artists of the next generation" (p. 616). With more than thirty acclaimed books for children and young adults spanning several genres (e.g., poetry, short stories, novels), Woodson *is* one of the most celebrated young adult authors today. Writing primarily contemporary realistic fiction, she raises questions about individuality, belonging, racial and class divisiveness, and activism while centering freedom and hope. Her books are ripe for discussions about minoritized groups, sexuality, social justice, and equity.

From the beginning, Woodson has been adept at exploring marginalized experiences in young adult literature, setting a trend that influenced other writers. Her second novel, *The Dear One* (1991), about twelve-year-old Afeni and Rebecca, a pregnant teen from Harlem, put Black girlhood and teen pregnancy in conversation during a time when few authors were approaching those topics.

Another early novel, *From the Notebooks of Melanin Sun* (1995), was praised for its depiction of a young man navigating Black male adolescence while trying to make sense of his mother's interracial relationship with a woman. The quote in this chapter's title—"We're all just people here"— sums up Woodson's cultural and literary impact across all her work and comes from *I Hadn't Meant to Tell You This* (1994), her sixth novel and the first of her books to receive major critical acclaim, winning a Coretta Scott King Award.

In 2006, Woodson received the Margaret A. Edwards Award honoring her outstanding lifetime contribution to writing for teens. The Edwards committee said, "Woodson's books are powerful, groundbreaking and very personal explorations of the many ways in which identity and friendship transcend the limits of stereotype" (YALSA, 2006).

To date, Woodson has received the biggest prizes in children's and young adult literature: the Newbery Honor Award, the National Book Award, the Coretta Scott King Author Award, and the Hans Christian Andersen Award. In 2010, she won the Catholic Library Association's St. Katharine Drexel Award for outstanding contribution to young adult literature, and in 2015 she won a NAACP Image Award for Outstanding Literary Work in Young Adult Fiction and the National Book Award for *Brown Girl Dreaming*.

More recently, in 2018, she was named the sixth National Ambassador for Young People's Literature in the United States, the Children's Literature Legacy Award recipient, and the laureate of the Astrid Lindgren Memorial Award, "the world's largest award for children's and young adult literature."

The jury that selected her as the Astrid Lindgren Memorial Award laureate said, "Jacqueline Woodson introduces us to resilient young people fighting to find a place where their lives can take root. In language as light as air, she tells stories of resounding richness and depth. Jacqueline Woodson captures a unique poetic note in a daily reality divided between sorrow and hope" (Swedish Arts Council, 2018). The 2020 Hans Christian Andersen Award jury noted that Woodson's books "feature lyrical language, powerful characters, and an abiding sense of hope" (Kantor, 2020).

The Astrid Lindgren Memorial Award jury's assessment of Woodson's work is consistent with how critics view it. She has been praised for her frank, well-crafted narratives that sensitively foreground issues of race, class, and sexuality while featuring characters that are complex, realistic, and memorable. Her writing has also been described as lyrical, graceful, and poignant. I asked Woodson what the recognition has meant to her, and she said, "I'm better known as a writer than I was before. . . . But I think the 'being known' thing is the most surprising. To have my work referenced, to see how many people have been exposed to it—this kind of thing was a long time coming and influenced greatly by the exposure brought on by the awards" (Hinton, 2012, p. 20). Woodson has reached celebrity status with appearances on such popular TV shows as *CBS This Morning*, *The Daily Show*, and *Late Night with Seth Myers*. Hollywood has also called on her to adapt novels into screenplays.

While Woodson is at work on a screenplay for her new adult novel, *Red at the Bone* (2019), a 2020 Lambda Literary Award finalist, her first book to be adapted for the screen was *Miracle's Boys* (2000), which won the Coretta Scott King Author Award. The novel and TV miniseries are about two teenaged brothers and their twenty-year-old older brother who puts his dream of attending MIT on hold to take care of them.

Clearly, Woodson's work is important and far-reaching, fulfilling Dr. Rudine Sims Bishop's prophecy that Woodson would become one of the most important literary voices of her generation.

CRITICAL DISCUSSION

Autobiography and family history are important parts of Woodson's oeuvre. She often writes stories inspired by her relationships with family members, particularly her grandmother. Grandmothers are central to many Black American families, and their commitment to raising their granddaughters is well documented in family studies and in children's literature scholarship (Hinton & Branyon, 2016). In *Show Way* (2005), a picture book that begins in the antebellum South, Woodson traces her maternal heritage and explores how her great-grandmother sewed quilts that led enslaved people to freedom.

Woodson draws on her rich family history and maternal lineage again in her memoir, *Brown Girl Dreaming* (2014), which garnered several awards. In it, Woodson explores what childhood was like for her during the 1960s while navigating different regions in the United States (e.g., segregated South Carolina and New York) all while developing the sensibilities (e.g., listening and observing) needed to become a writer. Critics have noted the book's skillful use of allusions (Bickmore, 2017) while depicting Black girlhood during the civil rights era of the 1960s and 1970s (McIlhagga, 2017).

Each of the five parts of *Brown Girl Dreaming* is filled with haikus and free verse and covers Woodson's birth in Ohio in 1963 through the end of elementary school in New York, taking readers on a journey with Woodson in and out of the South, where she is taught racial etiquette, conventions taught to Black and White children about how to speak and act around Whites (Ritterhouse, 2006).

In part one, Woodson reflects on her paternal grandparents' life in Ohio and emphasizes her paternal grandmother's southern heritage, one she shares with Woodson's mother, who misses her life in South Carolina. Yet, Woodson's father says, "No colored Buckeye in his right mind would ever want to go there [to the South]" (Woodson, 2014, p. 16). At odds, Woodson's mother moves their three children to a segregated town in South Carolina to live with her parents. The second part focuses on life with Woodson's grandparents, practicing Jehovah Witnesses who work as a teacher and dayworker (her grandmother) and as a foreman at a printing press (her grandfather).

While with them, in the third part of the book, Jackie develops and expands her consciousness of the world around her and realizes her gift for storytelling. Woodson's mother, who left her children in South Carolina while she pursued work in the North, retrieves them; thus, in the final two sections of the memoir, Woodson focuses on her childhood in New York, including her relationship with her fifth-grade teacher, one of the first to acknowledge and encourage her writing talent.

Brown Girl Dreaming explores Woodson's girlhood in the context of southern/northern landscapes and the activism of the 1960s; thus, classroom discussions about segregation, the Great Migration, and social justice are important. The book sparks discussions about how and why Woodson became a writer and whether place, particularly the South and migrating to the North, has meaning in relation to Black identity in general and Woodson's identity specifically. Not only do the characters migrate, but the text itself moves from the Midwest, to the South and North, and back to the South and West before finally settling in New York.

Griffin maintains Black migration texts are a "dominant form of African American cultural production" that typically include pivotal moments, such as a protagonist who is propelled to migrate from the South after an incident—usually one involving racism (1996, p. 4). The character is confronted with harsh realities and living conditions in the new location and struggles to adjust to the new locale's negative aspects, which often include the very types of racial injustice the protagonist hoped to have left behind. In some migration texts, the protagonist resists or embraces the South to adjust to and thrive in the new locale (Griffin, 1996).

Griffin's theory of pivotal moments of migration are found in Woodson's memoir as well. This is seen, for example, in "the leavers":

> They say the City is a place where diamonds
> speckle the sidewalk. Money
> falls from the sky.
> They say a colored person can do well going there.
> All you need is the fare out of Greenville.
> All you need is to know somebody on the other side,
> waiting to cross you over.
>
> Like the River Jordan
>
> and then you're in Paradise. (Woodson, 2014, p. 93)

The expectations and hopes of freedom and accomplishment are great. Once Woodson and her siblings join their mother in New York, the family encounters poor housing conditions, segregation, and racism. Indeed, the North is not paradise; and Jackie has an epiphany, like many migrants:

Maybe it's another New York City
the southerners talk about. Maybe that's where
there is money falling from the sky,
diamonds speckling
the sidewalks. (Woodson, 2014, p. 143)

She realizes the North also has obstacles, and some of them are like those experienced in the South.

Prevalent, too, are the "narrative conventions" of migration narratives, such as references to southern and northern racism, connections with ancestors, and experiences in urban areas such as "kitchenettes," "stoops," and "street corners" (Griffin, 1996). Yet, migrants also bring the South with them when they migrate:

And on Saturday nights more people
from Greenville came by
sitting and running their mouths
while the pots on the stove bubbled. (Woodson, 2014, p. 145, italics in original)

The migrant characters continue to embrace the South through food, language, and fellowship.

INSTRUCTIONAL ACTIVITIES

What follows are instructional activities that are inspired by Jacqueline Woodson's *Brown Girl Dreaming* and are aligned with the National Council of Teachers of English/International Reading Association standards, particularly standards involving reading works from a variety of periods and genres; conducting research and posing problems; synthesizing data from a variety of sources; valuing student contributions as members of a variety of literacy communities; and requiring spoken, written, and visual language as part of their communication practices.

Brown Girl Dreaming and the activities below can be used with students across grade levels. The activities promote literacy for pleasure and self-discovery, encourage freedom of expression, and develop research skills.

Individual Instruction

Hinton, Suh, O'Hearn, and Colón-Brown (2016) recommend ways to help students engage deeply with historical nonfiction like *Brown Girl Dreaming*.

One approach they suggest is questioning the author, popularized by Beck and McKeown (2002), which allows students to draw "conclusions about the author's unique experiences and how they might have influenced the text" (p. 40). Hinton et al. (2016) suggest that students should also read the author note in the book and consider several questions:

- Who wrote the book, when, and where?
- Why did the author write the book?
- What research did the author conduct to write the book?
- How can the author's approach to writing about the topic be imitated in our own nonfiction writing? (p. 40)

Along these same lines, while students read the Woodson memoir, ask them to keep a response journal in which they jot down questions they have; poems they like; allusions they notice (Bickmore, 2017); and details that help them understand the historical era, people, and events Woodson mentions (McIlhagga, 2017).

Brown Girl Dreaming can serve as an example or mentor text as students write their own memoir about their family history. Woodson's free verse and haikus can also be used as models for students' own poetry. Ask students to select one poem from *Brown Girl Dreaming* and use it as a model for writing about their own identity, family history, or environment. Ask them to set the poem to music or use some type of multimedia to share it with an audience. Similarly, encourage students to choose one poem from Woodson's memoir that they find significant and have them memorize it, record their performance of it, and share it with others.

Small-Group Instruction

Before Woodson began writing *Brown Girl Dreaming*, she could only recall fragments of her family's story. To fill in the gaps, she interviewed relatives and friends about her family's past and had informal conversations with them. Her dad "chimed in when he could" (Woodson, 2014, p. 324), and Maria, her best friend from childhood, filled in "gaps" and "helped the journey [writing process] along with pictures and stories" (Woodson, 2014, p. 325).

Woodson's childhood memories were prompted by travel to South Carolina and Ohio, where she visited grave sites and talked extensively to her aunt, a genealogist and family historian. Ask students to interview their family members about their history, particularly where and when migration was a factor.

In a small group, ask students to share one or two of their family's stories around migration and take note of their classmates' responses and questions. Encourage students to notice the types of details that seem to engage their classmates and use these observations as they draft a biopoem or vignette about how a family member's decision to migrate changed their life. Once the writing is complete, ask students to share it with the group.

History plays an important role in *Brown Girl Dreaming*. In fact, Woodson was born in 1963, a pivotal year that included events such as the March on Washington for Jobs and Freedom; the death of the four little girls as a result of a bombing during Sunday-morning services at the Sixteenth Street Baptist Church in Birmingham, Alabama; and other memorable moments. Ask students to create a timeline of historical events alluded to in the memoir and discuss what Woodson reveals about how the events affected her girlhood.

Woodson's verse novel includes different forms of poetry. Tell students about the Academy of American Poets' "Poem in Your Pocket" Day. Even if it isn't National Poetry Month, encourage students to find and select a poem they like, read it to each other in a small group, and carry it around with them for personal inspiration and to share with others, including on social media using the tag #pocketpoem.

As the National Ambassador for Young People's Literature, Woodson used a platform entitled "Reading = Hope x Change (What's Your Equation?)." As another small-group activity, students can discuss how reading can change our outlook on life. They can also brainstorm a list of texts that have encouraged or motivated them. Next, they can work together to create their own reading equation.

Whole-Class Instruction

Woodson often says the sparse, rhythmic language in her picture books is like poetry. Before introducing *Brown Girl Dreaming*, read *This Is the Rope: A Story from the Great Migration* (2013) and *Coming on Home Soon* (2004) aloud to the class. In *This Is the Rope*, point out the poetic language and the symbol of the rope passed on through generations, and lead students in a discussion about migration.

Next, read *Coming on Home Soon* and discuss how gender and social class might have affected who migrated and when. As the teacher, share your family's experiences with migration and ask students to do the same, noting the historical periods in which the migrations took place. Ask students to brainstorm reasons why people might have migrated within the United States in the past and then research the Great Migration to learn more.

Migration is such an important part of *Brown Girl Dreaming* and an important part of Black experiences and Black literature in general, so continue to discuss the importance of the migration theme throughout. As students read *Brown Girl Dreaming*, ask them to discuss instances when migration influences how Jackie sees the world as a budding storyteller.

Chronicling family history is another important part of *Brown Girl Dreaming*. Woodson has explored this in other books as well. For example, *Show Way* focuses on how Woodson's foremothers' love of literacy inspired her to become a writer. Students can read *Show Way* and other books by Woodson, such as *Coming on Home Soon* and *Locomotion* (2003), and discuss how Woodson's actual experiences link to those of her characters.

CONCLUSION

For nearly thirty years, Jacqueline Woodson has transformed the world of children's and young adult literature, making engaging and beautifully written books about diverse people available to scores of youths. Through her numerous accolades, she has championed reading, such as with her platform while serving as the National Ambassador for Young People's Literature: "Reading = Hope x Change (What's Your Equation?)."

Before campaigns such as We Need Diverse Books and #OwnVoices, Woodson advocated for readers and writers of color and taught and mentored many of them. Her books encourage frank yet civil conversations about race, class, sexuality, gender, and so much more. Woodson is undoubtedly a positive force in children's and young adult literature, helping readers find hope and declare that "we're all just people here."

SELECTED BIBLIOGRAPHY

Woodson, J. (1990). *Last summer with Maizon*. New York: Dell (reprint, Harcourt, 2002).
Woodson, J. (1991). *The dear one*. New York: Delacorte.
Woodson, J. (1994). *I hadn't meant to tell you this*. New York: Bantam Doubleday.
Woodson, J. (1995). *From the notebooks of Melanin Sun*. New York: Scholastic.
Woodson, J. (2000). *Miracle's boys*. New York: Putnam.
Woodson, J. (2003). *Locomotion*. New York: G. P. Putnam's Sons.
Woodson, J. (2004). *Coming on home soon* (E. B. Lewis, Illus.). New York: Putnam.
Woodson, J. (2005). *Show way* (H. Talbott, Illus.). New York: Putnam.
Woodson, J. (2008). *After Tupac and D Foster*. New York: Puffin.
Woodson, J. (2009). *Peace, locomotion*. New York: G. P. Putnam's Sons.

Woodson, J. (2012). *Beneath a meth moon*. New York: Nancy Paulsen Books.
Woodson, J. (2013). *This is the rope: A story from the Great Migration* (J. Ransome, Illus.). New York: Penguin.
Woodson, J. (2016). *Another Brooklyn*. New York: Amistad.
Woodson, J. (2019). *Red at the bone*. New York: Riverhead Books.

SELECT AWARDS FOR WOODSON'S OEUVRE

2018 Children's Literature Legacy Award (formerly Laura Ingalls Wilder Medal)
2018 Astrid Lindgren Memorial Award
2018 National Ambassador for Young People's Literature in the United States
2015 Young People's Poet Laureate
2010 Catholic Library Association's St. Katharine Drexel Award
2006 Margaret A. Edwards Award

SELECT AWARDS FOR *BROWN GIRL DREAMING*

2015 Robert F. Sibert Medal, Honor
2015 Newbery Medal Honor Book
2015 Coretta Scott King Award Winner, Author
2015 Claudia Lewis Award
2015 NAACP Image Award for Outstanding Literary Work in Young Adult Fiction
2014 *L.A. Times* Book Prize Finalist, Young Adult Literature
2014 National Book Award for Young People's Literature

SAMPLE SCHOLARLY WORKS: *BROWN GIRL DREAMING*

Abdur-Rahman, S. (2018). Spaces of the ancestor: Jacqueline Woodson and the long civil rights movement. *The Lion and the Unicorn, 42*(2), 180–197.
Anatol, G. L. (2016). *Brown girl dreaming*: A ghost story in the postcolonial goth tradition. *Children's Literature Association Quarterly, 41*(4), 403–419.
Howard, K. (2017). Collage, confession, and crisis in Jacqueline Woodson's *Brown girl dreaming*. *Children's Literature Association Quarterly, 42*(3), 326–344.

REFERENCES

Astrid Lindgren Memorial Award. (2018). American author Jacqueline Woodson is the laureate of Astrid Lindgren Memorial Award 2018. Retrieved from http://www.alma.se/en/Laureates/2018/.

Beck, I. L., & McKeown, M. G. (2002). Questioning the author: Making sense of social studies. *Educational Leadership, 60*(3), 44–47.

Bickmore, S. (2017). Second reaction: More dominant than the first: The power of memory in *Brown girl dreaming. First Opinions, Second Reactions, 10*(2). Retrieved from https://docs.lib.purdue.edu/fosr/vol10/iss2/11.

Bishop, R. S. (1992). Books from parallel cultures: New African American voices. *Horn Book Magazine, 68*(5), 616–620.

Griffin, F. J. (1996). *Who set you flowin'? The African American migration narrative.* Oxford, UK: Oxford University Press.

Hinton, K. (2012). Jacqueline Woodson: A writer's journey. *Library Media Connection, 30*(5), 20–21.

Hinton, K., & Branyon, A. (2016). Love is true-blue: Grandmothering in Rita Williams-Garcia's *One crazy summer* and *P.S. be eleven. Middle School Journal, 47*(4), 15–22.

Hinton, K., Suh, Y., O'Hearn, M., & Colón-Brown, L. (2016). Fostering habits of mind: A framework for reading historical nonfiction illustrated by the case of *Hitler Youth. Voices from the Middle, 23*(3), 38–44.

Kantor, E. (2020, May 4). Jacqueline Woodson and Albertine win 2020 Hans Christian Andersen Awards. *Publisher's Weekly.* Retrieved from https://www.publish ersweekly.com/pw/by-topic/childrens/childrens-authors/article/83231-jacqueline -woodson-and-albertine-win-2020-hans-christian-andersen-awards.html.

McIlhagga, K. K. A. (2017). First opinion: Waking up: *Brown girl dreaming* in 2017. *First Opinions, Second Reactions, 10*(2). Retrieved from https://docs.lib.purdue. edu/fosr/vol10/iss2/10.

Ritterhouse, J. (2006). *Growing up Jim Crow: How Black and White Southern children learned race.* Chapel Hill: University of North Carolina Press.

Swedish Arts Council. (2018). American author Jacqueline Woodson is the laureate of Astrid Lindgren memorial award. Retrieved from https://alma.se/en/laureates /jacqueline-woodson/.

Woodson, J. (2014). *Brown girl dreaming.* New York: Nancy Paulsen Books.

YALSA. (2006). 2006 Margaret A. Edwards Award winner Jacqueline Woodson. Retrieved from https://www.ala.org/yalsa/2006-margaret-edwards-award-winner -jacqueline-woodson.

Chapter 2

Coming of Age and Confronting Sexual Identity in Jacqueline Woodson's *From the Notebooks of Melanin Sun*

Tammy Szafranski and Steven T. Bickmore

In chapter 1, KaaVonia Hinton outlines Jacqueline Woodson's impact on the world of children's and young adult literature, including winning the National Book Award in 2015 for *Brown Girl Dreaming* (2015) and serving as the sixth National Ambassador for Young People's Literature in the United States from 2018 to 2020. Woodson writes beautiful stories about families, friendships, and finding acceptance in the world. It would be too simple to say she writes coming-of-age stories. While this is true, she doesn't shy away from the difficult topics of family trauma, racial injustice, and sexual identity.

In classic Woodson fashion, her 1995 novel, *From the Notebooks of Melanin Sun* (1995), covers a wide range of themes, including such sensitive topics as homophobia, racism, and class inequality, as well as more traditional young adult literature material, including sexuality, friendship, and parent-child conflict. The book's central focus, however, is on the relationship between Melanin and his single mother, Encanta Cedar (referred to as EC throughout the narrative).

For the teacher seeking to work with this book, the key concept on which the text focuses is the power that words have to hurt or to heal. This is particularly evident in the fact that the reader enters the narrative through the reflections of thirteen-year-old (soon to be fourteen) Melanin Sun, as recorded in his notebooks ("notebooks," he asserts—not diaries. "Girls keep diaries."). And just like many adolescents his age, Melanin finds that "the world turns upside down when you are thirteen going on fourteen," and indeed, in Melanin's world, it has (Woodson, 2010, p. 70).

CRITICAL DISCUSSION

At the end of summer, before school starts, Melanin's thoughts are consumed by two things: spending time with his friends Ralphy and Sean and dating Angie, a girl with whom he is developing a shy and somewhat awkward relationship. At the heart of these preoccupations is the fear of perception and appearance, in particular, the concern that he will not appear "masculine" enough to others and be labeled a homosexual.

Melanin is especially concerned about this because he enjoys stamp collecting and studying endangered species, hobbies about which his friends frequently tease him: "I knew it was faggy to collect stamps, but I didn't care. It was something I liked so long as I didn't start wanting to kiss on Ralphael or Sean, I was okay. A long time ago I figured out that there were two kinds of 'faggy.' There's the kind that . . . really isn't super macho and has notebooks to write stuff down in. Not diaries. Notebooks. Girls keep diaries. The other kind of 'faggy' was the really messed up kind" (Woodson, 2010, pp. 18–19).

The stabilizing force in Melanin's life throughout all this is his single mother, EC. Because Melanin knows nothing about his father ("He moved off somewhere and said maybe they could stay in touch"), he has grown up in a world inhabited only by her. This results in a particularly intense emotional connection between the two, as they have been relying on one another his entire life: "Me and Mama sipping iced tea while the sun pours into the living room, turning us and everything around us gold. This is all anybody needs to be happy" (Woodson, 2010, p. 9).

This connection, however, also leads Melanin to feel a sense of ownership toward EC, even though she has her own life and activities, such as putting herself through law school and working out at the gym. She also periodically brings dates home for Melanin to meet, but nothing has ever been serious, and this prompts Melanin to think nothing will ever change: "So what if Mama's had a little something going on the side. It wasn't anything important. She was a grown-up. If she wanted a boyfriend for a little while, it wasn't my business. He'd be gone soon enough. Then it'd be like it was before. Mama and me talking quietly in the kitchen, being close. Being there for each other" (Woodson, 2010, p. 22).

But this mother-son harmony becomes suddenly dissonant when EC admits to Melanin that she is a lesbian and that she has been dating a fellow law student, Kirsten, without his knowledge, for quite some time. This aspect of the story is especially prescient and still remarkably relevant. While the narrative trope of the teenager dealing with his or her own homosexuality is more commonly explored in young adult literature, Woodson takes on the task of exploring how a teenager deals with a parent's homosexuality.

In this case, Melanin's confusion about his own sexual feelings toward Angie, as well as his fear of appearing "emasculated" in front of his male friends, drives his reactions to his mother's admission—often in harsh and unfair terms: "'You're a dyke! A dyke! A dyke! . . . That's why nobody wants you. Nobody. That's why my father disappeared and even the ugly guys didn't come back!'" (Woodson, 2010, p. 58).

While the term *dyke* is somewhat dated, the overall essence of the slur remains, and the effects of hurtful names and terms can be explored in classroom discussions and various activities like the one that appears at the end of this chapter in the Before Reading Activity section. The key is to allow students a safe space in which to examine some of the negative and harmful words commonly used to bully or tease people and to then allow students time to reflect on why it is not kind or appropriate—even dangerous to others—to use such terms.

As for Melanin, aside from having to deal with his mother's homosexuality, he also struggles to overcome his own racial prejudices toward his mother's lover, as she is a White woman. His critiques allow for an exploration of stereotypes and cultural norms, as his initial assessment of Kirsten is framed largely on perceptions of White privilege as seen through the lens of popular culture: "This woman wasn't fine or a sister. She was white. White white. Like shampoo commercial girl white but with glasses. And those straight white-people teeth you know must have cost her parents a million dollars in dental bills. She had that shimmery white-people hair that has a whole lot of shades of brown and blond running through it and a dimple in one cheek" (Woodson, 2010, p. 29).

For the bulk of the narrative, Melanin wrestles with the dilemma of loving his mother and being angry at her for what he perceives as an attempted coup on his social life. On one hand, he knows that his mother is his only real family ("Everybody but Mama and me died before I was born"); on the other hand, he catastrophizes about what the outside world will think: "I'm scared the whole world is going to know. Maybe they do already"(Woodson, 2010, p. 65).

These shifts are beautifully detailed in the reflections he records in his notebooks. From a literary perspective, it is in these reflections that the reader connects with Melanin's confusion in a more profound way, as he tries to imagine himself out of his situation by placing others in his shoes: "What is this? What makes life so crazy? How come it's her of all the mothers in the world that has to be a dyke? How come it can't be Ralph's mom? Or Sean's? Or even Angie's?" (Woodson, 2010, p. 98).

But, of course, wishing does not change Melanin's circumstances, and it is in his friends' widely differing responses to his circumstances that he begins to understand that the world is actually far more complex than he previously realized. From an educational perspective, this gives teachers a chance to discuss the textual clues that foreshadow each character's response. From a narrative perspective, Sean's reaction is the most interesting because it is fueled by tension and jealousy surrounding Melanin's burgeoning relationship with Angie: "Angie and I walked bumping shoulders. Ralph and Sean gave us glances but didn't say anything. Sean was glaring. Maybe he was jealous" (Woodson, 2010, p. 95).

This scene is quickly followed by Ralph suggesting that Melanin and Angie should go on a double date. This sets off a flurry of angry dialogue from Sean, who outs Melanin's mother in purposefully inflammatory terms: "Why don't you take her out on a double date with your mama and that dyke she's seeing?" (Woodson, 2010, p. 96). Melanin subsequently punches Sean, and in the ensuing fight he is forced to acknowledge that perhaps his friendship with Sean is not as important to him as he once thought it was: "Maybe when we get older, people will forget all this and ask me, 'Whatever happened to your homeboy, Sean?' And I'll have to say I don't know because I don't, and I probably never will. So it ends like this" (Woodson, 2010, p. 111).

On the opposite side, Melanin finds that his relationship with Ralph remains unaffected and perhaps even grows stronger. Students may find Ralph's response sympathetic and even humorous: "'Oh . . . it's no big deal you know. Like, what goes on with your mother doesn't have anything to do with anybody else, right? . . . [Mama] saw EC day before yesterday in the store and she looked happier than anything. Mama said she should go out and find herself a woman if that's what it's all about'" (Woodson, 2010, pp. 107–109).

It may be helpful at this point to conduct a discussion about what the term *ally* means in response to LGBTQ issues, particularly because the subsequent responses of both Ralph and Sean represent opposite ends of the spectrum. Sean uses homophobia to embarrass and divide Melanin from his peers for goals that lay outside gender politics; Ralph, on the other hand, being devoid of any goal outside of maintaining an important friendship, becomes a de facto ally for Melanin and his mother.

There is also a suggestion in the novel that family perspectives play a role in how the boys see sexual identity. Sean's mother forbids him from ever associating with Melanin again. Ralph's mother, on the other hand, not only accepts the situation without any emotional response but clearly notes that as long as Melanin's mother is happy, that is all that matters. At this point the discussion on the definition of *ally* might well move into allowing students to come up with their own definitions, including such things as "acceptance and support of loved ones and friends."

The most essential turning point in the novel comes when Melanin's mother invites Kirsten to spend the day with them at Jones Beach. While

Melanin wants to remain cold to Kirsten, he finds that he is unable to continue projecting a stoic exterior because he begins to come to a very adult realization: Kirsten is just another person. In a rather humorous exchange in which the two are sitting on the end of Melanin's bed, Kirsten tries to define *gayness* for Melanin in nonloaded, nonpolitical terms:

"Who is your friend?"

I thought for a moment and told her it was Ralphael.

"Do you like going to the movies with him?"

I nodded.

"And spending time with him?"

I nodded again, not knowing what she was getting at.

"Okay, now would you like to kiss Ralphael?"

"No!"

She threw her hands up. "Well, that's the difference!" (Woodson, 2010, p. 117)

When Melanin tries to point out that boys aren't supposed to want to kiss other boys, Kirsten lightly bounces back, "Who says?" It is this same grounded honesty between them that allows Melanin to come to see Kirsten as a person who, like his mother, has been through her own share of hardships: "I wanted to ask Kirsten what it felt like to still have a family alive somewhere and not be able to talk to them. Did it feel like it did with my father? Hollow and empty sometimes?" (Woodson, 2010, p. 123).

By the end of the novel, Melanin has not completely resolved his feelings, but he has moved into a place where he is able to assert that family is the most important thing in his life—regardless of what it looks like or how it is defined. He has also grown to acknowledge that what other people think no longer matters quite so much to him: "We sat there without saying anything for a long time. People passing by must have wondered about us—how strange we looked together—a black guy and a white woman sitting silently staring out at the water. But I didn't care anymore what people were thinking. Some part of me was starting to move inside of myself, shutting out all those nosey eyes and nasty things people can think to say" (Woodson, 2010, p. 124).

INSTRUCTIONAL ACTIVITIES

From an instructional standpoint, *Melanin Sun* is a boon for English language arts teachers. The book not only provides ample opportunity to reflect on language and vocabulary but also explores these subjects through the written activities of the main character. This is a prime opportunity for English teachers, specifically, to fully engage with the writing process and to help their students develop critical thinking and writing skills through individual and group projects. And because the book relies heavily on character-derived definitions of terms, it also allows teachers the opportunity to address important composition skills in an engaging, text-driven way.

Before Reading

Without question, one of the most important aspects of the novel is the way that words are used negatively and positively to both hurt and heal. Before students begin reading this text, it is important to open a discussion about the subjective meaning of words versus their objective definitions. This learning directive can be achieved through individual, small-group, and whole-class activities.

Individual

To help individual students realize the importance of the different meanings words carry through denotation and connotation, context, and tone, teachers might conduct a few mini lessons that help students remember how words can shift meaning. For example, the word *liberal* might immediately divide a class if placed in a political context but would instantly unify that same class if students were being offered a "liberal" portion of ice cream. To emphasize how context changes a word's meaning, there are several activities that students can explore individually to see if they can readily make the meaning shift.

Teachers might begin this exercise by demonstrating the difference between denotation and connotation. For example, the word *baggage* means one thing at an airport and quite another in a session with a school counselor. A common activity is to ask students to consider words that might describe something similar but carry different circumstantial meanings. For example, words such as *clique, group, gang, club,* or *team* change definition based on the circumstances in which they are used.

Teachers might consider asking students how these words are similar and how they are different. They might then want to have students use each one in a sentence to demonstrate how the words carry different meanings.

Since the book begins with Melanin contemplating his own masculinity, teachers might have students focus on words that imply different connotations about sexual identity. A word of caution is important here. Such words are often used to bully or demean other students. As the class begins a study of *From the Notebooks of Melanin Sun* or other books that address bullying and marginalization, teachers might wish to review the classroom expectations for how students treat one another.

At this point, instructors should check for understanding and make sure students can determine how words shift meaning depending on context. These small beginning activities can be expanded by asking students to create a list of five to ten words from the novel. Students can look specifically at how Woodson uses different words to create tone and nuanced meaning during the course of the book.

Small-Group Activity

One way to have students examine tone and nuance would be to provide students with a list of words from the novel and have them create definitions based on how Woodson presents them and how their own personal experiences might lead them to understand these words differently (see textbox 2.1).

TEXTBOX 2.1   EXPLORING DENOTATION AND CONNOTATION THROUGH COLLABORATIVE EXPERIENCE

In this activity students will be asked to draw on their own experiences with language and how the word was used in the text. For example, Melanin wonders about his masculinity and uses the word *fag*. The teacher could take the opportunity to explore the various dictionary definitions of the word. Then the students could examine how the word is used in various cultural contexts.

1. Break students into groups of three or four.
2. Provide each group with paper and pens; alternatively, students can be placed into breakout rooms online and given a link to a virtual document.
3. The paper/documents can either have words prewritten on them, or students can be shown a list on a projector, whiteboard, or PowerPoint presentation.
4. Some suggested words from the text include the following: family, alone/loneliness, friendship, writing, masculinity/femininity, love, and home. Of course, teachers should explore the text and make their own selections as well.
5. Give the students ample time to discuss the concepts based on the number of terms you have provided for them. They should then come up with a bulleted list of definitions for each word. Make sure they write these out on the paper or type them in the document so they can be shared or saved.

Whole-Class Activity

The following whole-class jigsaw activity builds on the small-group project. This requires students to be part of at least two groups during the class session. In the first group, students will discuss a topic and become "experts" on how their group defines and understands that subject.

After the first round, students will leave their first group as an expert representative and join a new group of other experts. In this second round, each expert takes a turn sharing or instructing others about the results of their first group's discussion. After all members have taken a turn, the group can then discuss how each group's findings were the same or different. For instructors seeking to use this method, more information about conducting a jigsaw activity can be found with a simple Google search; in addition, many English methods textbooks will provide further assistance and suggestions.

For *Melanin Sun*, teachers can use this activity to push student thinking further by having them generate a list of words they encountered that have been used to bully, tease, or make fun of others. This list need not be extensive; three or four terms would be sufficient. The groups should then record the words and explain how they have been used to hurt others.

Each person in the group will prepare notes and be ready to share the results of their first group's discussion with the next group. Form the second group. Within the new groups, each student takes a turn explaining why the word was hurtful. Because this may be sensitive for some students, they should be allowed to choose only one word from their lists, even if the instructor views all three or four terms.

During Reading

Melanin Sun frequently refers to his notebooks as the only things that are "mine. All mine" (Woodson, 2010, p. 88). Because writing is such an important activity both for the protagonist in the novel and for students in real life, this project is designed to help organize the writing process while still allowing space for reflection and creative activity. That said, the main focus of this activity needs to be on written composition.

Individual

Divide the novel into several sections, and have students create either a hard-copy or virtual notebook. Ask individual students to find impactful moments in the text that touch on their own experiences or cause them to feel empathy for Melanin's situation. If students write freely about their feelings as they react and respond to Melanin, they can track their own emotions throughout their reading of the novel. This will prepare them to think more deeply about the critical issues of family, parent/child relationships, and wrestling with queer identities.

A helpful way of doing this is to have students prelabel the sections of their notebook. For example, one section might be labeled *parent–child conflicts*, the next might be *conflict with friends*, and a third could perhaps be *conflict with self*. If the book is divided into nine sections and the students rotate the three suggested ideas, this will provide them the opportunity to respond to each category three times and reconsider and revisit their own attitudes about each topic as they progress through the book. This activity allows students to write free responses and deal with the literary aspects of characterization within a novel.

Small Groups

Using their own notebooks as a guide to how they have been responding to the various issues that arise from reading the text, students can work in small groups to further articulate their thinking about key themes. The three topics listed in textbox 2.2 (important words, heroes and villains, and exploring imagery) can guide small-group discussions at several points along the way. Thus, readers are forced to consider more than just the beginning and end of the book, thereby giving more weight to what happens in the narrative along the way as the plot and the characters develop.

Too often teachers spend excessive classroom time introducing a book and even more time discussing how themes, plot devices, and characters are brought to a resolution after the students have "finished" reading a novel. In reality, not all students read the books teachers assign. Providing well-designed activities placed at intermittent points while students read a text encourages them to remain interested, holds them accountable, and helps them collect textual evidence that might be used for final essays, tests, or concluding presentations. The suggestions in textbox 2.2 will help students focus as they read.

TEXTBOX 2.2   JIGSAW ACTIVITIES: IMPORTANT WORDS, HEROES AND VILLAINS, AND EXPLORING IMAGERY

The following three activities—Important Words, Heroes and Villains, and Exploring Imagery—can be done two or three times while reading the story. A teacher may choose to have each small group concentrate on the same activity for the first "during reading" pause and then move to the next activity during the next reading break. It might be just as useful to have different groups tackle a different activity and then share with other groups through the use of jigsaw activities or as reports to the whole class.

(continued)

TEXTBOX 2.2   (*CONTINUED*)

- Important Words: Have students choose important words from the reading section and write about how or why they are important to the text.
- Heroes and Villains: Throughout various sections of the book, Melanin views certain characters differently based on his perceptions of how they act and react to him and to his circumstances. People do this in real life as well. Have students explore how or why Melanin's views on certain characters shift and change. Is he seeing this character fairly, or are his judgments clouded by his own prejudice? Have students use quotes from the text to support their ideas.
- Exploring Imagery: Melanin has an artistic soul, and this is frequently reflected in his descriptions of people, places, and things in the novel. Have students write about why a particular image described by Melanin is meaningful to them. They can also include a picture or artistic rendering of the scene or image.

Whole Class

Brainstorming as a class, students can explore terms they have encountered through their reading and have felt compelled to write about. Have they found situations and/or conflicts between characters that have made them uncomfortable? Are there scenes that have forced them to reconsider their attitudes? Have they felt compelled to contemplate their own interactions with their parents, siblings, or friends?

As a homework assignment, students can be asked to review their journals and come prepared to share a passage, theme, or idea that has captured their attention. When they arrive, students can be asked to share one of their preselected ideas. It is important to validate all responses, and it is okay if a student mentions the same thing as another student. In fact, important ideas and passages might be cataloged on the board several times.

Once everyone has contributed, the teacher should ask for volunteers to suggest important themes that have not yet been mentioned. Not every idea can be discussed completely in a twenty- to thirty-minute time frame, so a technique called Vegas Voting can be employed to add fun to the selection of the primary discussion topics. Using this technique, students are given three sticky notes and are invited to visit the board and cast their vote for the topic(s) they would like to hear discussed. They may cast their vote more than once on the same topic; so, for example, a single student might vote three times for "masculinity."

When all the votes have been tallied and the topics selected, the teacher should ask students to take a few moments to write down their thoughts on the discussion topics. This gives students thinking time, so they will be more likely to contribute their ideas to the discussion. Since discussion rarely includes all the students in a classroom, teachers can collect these notes so that all students can be given credit for participating, whether they have spoken in class or not.

An additional action would be to require students to add these discussion notes to their journals. With these, they can begin to create a "commonplace book" similar to one designed by a primary character in Michael Ondaatje's *The English Patient* (1992). Then, as students add notes and other materials to their journal, it becomes a multigenre project (Romano, 2000). Other materials can be added to these journals; for example, students can add the results of any Google searches they may have done while reading and any other written notes or responses to the text. In essence, this becomes their version of Melanin's notebooks.

After Reading

The focus of *From the Notebooks of Melanin Sun* is on how the act of writing expresses, channels, and heals the soul, and the author, Jacqueline Woodson, frequently discusses how this is true for her in real life. In the 2010 rerelease of the novel, an interview with Woodson is reprinted at the back of the book. When asked about why she writes, Woodson frankly replies, "Because it makes me happy" (Woodson, 2010, p. 130). When asked when she will stop writing, she answers, "When I stop breathing" (Woodson, 2010, p. 133).

Using this as an inspiration for your students, you can have them do the following activity, designed to help them think about their own writing process and about how and why they write.

Individual

Students can be asked to conduct a small research project on an author. Since the focus of this book series is African American writers, it would be appropriate to use those listed in the Coretta Scott King John Steptoe Award, which is sponsored by the American Library Association. This particular award was established in 1996, and many of its winners are featured in this book series. Other honorees include David Barclay Moore, Alicia D. Williams, Nicola Yoon, and Tracy Deonn.

Research projects take many forms, and one manageable way to accomplish this is to provide a list of guiding questions that help students explore their chosen author's attitudes about writing and the creative process. Students can be asked to read and report on a work by the author and to imitate the author's style in a written passage. For a more directed entrance into this research activity, see textbox 2.3.

TEXTBOX 2.3   WHO IS THIS AUTHOR?

Pick or assign an author from the Steptoe winners.

1. What year did the author win the award, and what book was cited as an exemplar of their work?
2. Find basic information about the author's life.
3. Reference an interview with the author.
4. Find a book review from a reputable source (*New York Times*, *Los Angeles Times*, *Kirkus Reviews*, etc.).
5. From these sources, students should make statements or assertions about the author's feelings about writing and writing practices, answering questions such as the following:

   a. How does he or she feel about the act of writing?
   b. How does he or she choose the times and places that he or she writes about?
   c. How does he or she decide what to write about (subject matter)?
   d. How does he or she deal with writer's block?

Have the students then do a comparison between their chosen author's practices and attitudes about writing and their own practices and attitudes. There can be a class discussion or presentation component to this assignment, but make sure that students are engaging with the composing process at some point in this project.

Students might submit their findings in a written essay or in a digital format using a PowerPoint, a web page, a blog post, a Prezi presentation, or another digital avenue that might appeal to them. Once again, the teacher should ensure that students use both traditional and experimental forms of writing using a process-oriented approach.

Small Group

A possible small-group activity is to ask students to consider how masculinity or gender performance might have played out in other books they have read, either as part of their schooling or on their own. Common classroom texts include such works as *To Kill a Mockingbird*, *The Giver*, and *The Great Gatsby*, but extending this to books they have read on their own opens the field of exploration and relocates critical thinking outside the classroom. Students may choose to examine how Scout or Daisy are portrayed in their canon reading (*To Kill a Mockingbird*), but they may also want to discuss how Hermione Granger is viewed or treated differently from Harry and Ron and, by extension, how Harry and Ron are treated differently from one another (Harry Potter series).

Another version of this assignment is to ask students to consider how the Disney "princess" movies affirm or question gender roles in terms of action, motivation, and expectation. Students can consider how the motivations of Elsa in *Frozen* are different from those of Ariel in *The Little Mermaid*; what does this tell viewers about how society imparts value to female identity? Another interesting comparison involves the way the characters of Mulan (*Mulan*) and Belle (*Beauty and the Beast*) choose to handle their problematic situations, even though their motivation (to save their fathers) is arguably the same. Moreover, why are there no Disney "prince" movies?

To accomplish this activity, it will be necessary to have students do some work on their own before class. First, students should be divided into groups of three or four. Each group must then decide what book or movie they want to discuss. Once they have decided this, they can be asked to write a brief rationale on why they made their particular choice, citing three reasons (this establishes core competencies). They can then fill out a chart that is divided into the following areas:

1. How does the character sees himself or herself?
2. How do other characters in the book see him or her?
3. Does gender influence how the character sees himself or herself?
4. Does gender influence the way the other characters see him or her?
5. Does gender influence how the reader views the character?

Once these charts have been filled out, one student from each group can be asked to share her or his findings with the class. The teacher may also choose to put important or repeated words that appear in the various presentations on the board or screen and can either have students write about the ones they feel are most essential or conduct a full-room discussion on them.

Whole Class

Writing can be an intimidating activity for students to engage with. Melanin Sun has no such fear, and it is a good text to use to help students move beyond their reluctance to write. One way to achieve this is to use the author's interview and her reflections on the text to open a discussion about writing and writing practices. The following activity can be used to begin a classroom conversation on writing:

1. Teachers should first read through the Woodson interview with students.
2. Students can then discuss Woodson's answers in relation to the novel and in relation to how they feel about writing.

3. Some questions to pose to students include the following:

   a. What kinds of writing do students do in their everyday lives?
   b. What do students think "good" writing is?
   c. What do students do to prepare for writing an assignment, if anything?
   d. How do they think writing can be beneficial to them in their everyday lives—both in the present and in the future?
   e. What are their greatest concerns and fears with regard to writing?

4. Teachers can use this as a kind of diagnostic going forward to help students feel less anxious about the writing process.

An activity like this one can help students evaluate their own attitudes toward the writing process. This can be especially useful if a teacher plans to incorporate memoir writing in the unit that follows this one. In fact, a good starting point is for students to analyze their own journals they have been keeping as they were reading and studying *From the Notebooks of Melanin Sun*.

CONCLUSION

From the Notebooks of Melanin Sun is a multilayered text, and teachers can use many different activities and approaches to investigate this work with their students. Perhaps the novel's greatest strength is its complexity in terms of theme, content, and character because, in a sense, it operates essentially the same way life does. The key for teachers is to use the book's primary focus on writing as a way to manage these complexities and to help their students see writing as yet another tool to use as they struggle to explore and understand their own complex experiences.

REFERENCES

Ondaatje, M. (1992). *The English patient: A novel*. New York: Knopf.

Romano, T. (2000). *Blending genre, altering style: Writing multigenre papers*. Portsmouth, NH: Boynton/Cook, Heinemann.

Sumara, D. J. (1996). *Private readings in public: Schooling the literary imagination*. New York: Peter Lang.

Woodson, J. (2010). *From the notebooks of Melanin Sun*. New York: Puffin.

Woodson, J. (2014). *Brown girl dreaming*. New York: Nancy Paulsen Books.

Chapter 3

A Life Revealed

Angela Johnson's The First Part Last *and the Transformational Power of the Personal Narrative*

Matt Skillen

Angela Johnson, an Alabama native and Ohio resident, is an internationally renowned poet and author who has published books that speak to the very soul of a generation. Johnson's books elevate ordinary characters to capture the essence of life that envelops readers of all ages and backgrounds.

Widely celebrated for her picture books (e.g., *A Sweet Smell of Roses, I Dream of Trains, Julius,* and *Shoes Like Ms. Alice*), Johnson's collaborations with illustrators have included E. B. Lewis, James Ransome, David Soman, Loren Long, and Dav Pilkey. With beautiful verse, Johnson's stories of friendship, hope, and love are framed with timeless illustrations that transport readers of all ages to times and places not long forgotten. Each book conveys a story worth telling, and each story leaves a lasting impression.

As a novelist, Johnson creates characters that are truly unique and positions them in spaces where they must navigate the boundaries of life—through loss, separation, and grief. Through these characters and their stories, readers are introduced to a wide variety of people they have never met, yet they resemble the people we see every day in our work, in our schools, and in our communities. They are authentic, and their pain is real.

CRITICAL DISCUSSION

A five-time Coretta Scott King Award winner, Johnson has clearly made a lasting impact on the publishing industry. She is a Michael L. Printz Award winner, an Ezra Jack Keats New Author Award winner, and a 2003 MacArthur Fellow. She has written more than forty books, and each is timeless. Johnson is prolific, and the characters she creates are real and relatable. She is sensitive to family dynamics and writes about the stories she sees unfolding in the lives of those around her. She has written beautiful, tough stories and has expanded to also write about African American history, shedding light on remarkable people that everyone should know about.

When asked about her interest in writing stories about young adults, Johnson says, "Kids and teens are so much more interesting than adults. Life is happening when you are a teenager. One minute you're a child, the next you're allowed to go out in the world by yourself. Who knows what will happen?" (A. Johnson, personal interview, n.d.). This unexpectedness of adolescence is not only a theme of her writing; it is a foundation. Life swirls around her main characters as they move through each story she creates.

Johnson's storytelling isn't haphazard. There is intentionality in her craft as she attempts to connect with her readers. She says, "I want them to come to a safe place when they are reading my books—even if the story is tumultuous. I want my voice to be one that they can count on for a good story and maybe even take away something that might hold them in good stead. But mainly, I want to connect" (A. Johnson, personal interview, February 8, 2009). The purposeful attempt to connect her stories to her readers comes with a brilliant stroke of artistic genius, and her brilliance will hit all readers when they pick up *The First Part Last* (2003).

The First Part Last is the second installment of the massively popular Heaven series, published between 1998 and 2010. The series centers on three different stories that orbit around Heaven, Ohio—a fictitious quaint small town near Lake Erie. The gravitational pull of Heaven is stronger in some of the stories than others, but this setting plays an important role in defining Johnson's main characters throughout the three-part series.

Bobby, the main character of *The First Part Last*, grows up in Brooklyn, New York, a completely different setting compared to Heaven. Bobby is an impulsive sixteen-year-old with a world of opportunity before him. He is creative and funny. He enjoys going to the beach with his friends and finding new walls to spray paint—a public gallery of sorts for his latest mural. In Bobby, Johnson creates a character that is immediately likable and unforgettable, but there is one thing about Bobby that makes him truly unique—he's a father.

In a move of creative genius, Johnson crafts a story around teenage pregnancy that is rarely told. *The First Part Last* disrupts the stereotypical narrative of the "absent father," and this perspective can be profound for adolescents. Johnson shines a light on this teenager as he assumes the awesome responsibilities of raising a daughter. Through Bobby, we get a glimpse of the life of a single teenaged father, and our introduction to Bobby and his daughter, Feather, in the first few pages of the book is absolutely breathtaking.

The first chapter opens with Bobby remembering that his mother routinely told him that he didn't really sleep through the night until he was eight. As he sits with his own newborn daughter, tired from the sleepless nights, he gets it. In a fitting tribute to his mother, Bobby sees the work that his mother must have put in to provide for him. He says,

> So last week when it looked like Feather probably wasn't ever going to sleep through the night, I lay her on my stomach and breathed her in. My daughter is eleven days old.
>
> And that sweet new baby smell . . . the smell of baby shampoo, formula, and my mom's perfume. It made me cry like I hadn't since I was a little kid. (Johnson, 2003, p. 4)

Captured in this simple, elegant introduction are two prevailing themes that develop throughout the novel. Bobby is stuck somewhere between childhood and adulthood. Throughout the story, he struggles to balance on the thin line between these two perspectives of his life. On the one hand, he is a teenager in high school, and all around him he witnesses people his age doing the normal things teenagers do—playing video games, hanging out on the street corner with friends after school, laughing, living carefree. On the other hand, he is holding on to his daughter, Feather, while she holds on to him. He bends his will to provide the very best he can for her, though he doesn't quite know what that is. And this is no small thing.

In this story, Johnson creates a single African American father that challenges the stereotype of the absent father that is advanced in many social narratives. The profound relationship between a father and daughter is amplified as Bobby navigates the uncertainty of raising a child.

Furthermore, an interesting dynamic that emerges from this theme is Bobby's natural paternal instinct to protect his daughter. While he is still developing his understanding of masculinity, he is at the same time attempting to raise, guide, and protect an innocent illustration of femininity as well. This creates noticeable tension throughout the story as Bobby attempts to navigate this new normal in his life—not young, but certainly not old; not a boy, but certainly not yet a man.

The second theme that runs through the book is a tension that exists between *then* and *now*. The novel bounces between a time before Feather was born and after, before Bobby became a father and after. Because the novel unravels Bobby's story in this way, readers struggle to get their arms all the way around how Bobby finds himself in this position—trying to raise a daughter while finishing high school.

Johnson's nonlinear approach draws the reader in to experience the disorienting confusion that Bobby feels. The reader bounces back and forth in time, leading up to a remarkable turning point in Bobby's story, when he ascends from childhood and captures adulthood. Furthermore, because this story is told from Bobby's first-person perspective, we arrive with Bobby at that moment, and we get to experience this transition firsthand.

Embedded in this first-person, nonlinear narrative are beautifully written personal accounts of a teenager who experiences great triumphs and tragedies through the transition of his life. These high and low points serve as important lessons and reflection points. Take for instance a scene in part three when Bobby finds himself in real trouble:

> I gotta catch a break.
>
> The cop who brings me in is on the phone, and looking through some file like she's got nothing to do but slowly look through paper.
>
> We walk up tiled stairs past gray walls to a squad room.
>
> She points to a chair and says, "Sit, kid."
>
> I sit.
>
> And when I look at the clock over the window facing a brick wall, I feel my stomach turning over. 7:30 P.M. Coco must be buggin' with my mom beside her, burning up every phone on the island. (Johnson, 2003, p. 69)

In this scene, Bobby is picked up by a police officer for spray painting a brick wall. Earlier in the day, he was riding high when a neighbor, Coco, offered to watch Feather while Bobby ran off to school. This convenient support saved Bobby a great deal of time on this particular day, and for a moment, he had the feeling that something might just go his way. He felt confident, so confident that he decided to try to paint before school started. That, as it turns out, was a mistake in judgment.

Bobby's stomach turns as he looks at the clock in the police station. It is 7:30 p.m., and his baby has been with Coco for twelve hours. He has no way to contact Coco. In that moment he is sling-shot back into adulthood with the realization that he is no longer an island unto himself. His daughter needs him.

Toward the end of the novel, we read of the moment Bobby decides to raise Feather himself instead of following through with the plans he and Nia, Bobby's girlfriend, made to put their baby up for adoption after she was born. Nia doesn't want to be a mother; she makes this very clear in her conversations with Bobby. Near the end of her pregnancy, Nia is rushed to the hospital. Johnson doesn't tell us exactly why Nia is rushed to the hospital, but the clues she provides indicate it is serious. The medical team delivers Feather.

Amid the sudden crisis that Bobby's and Nia's families are now thrust into, Bobby sits looking at the adoption papers. The fog of confusion clears for a moment. Bobby hears the social worker assigned to the adoption say, "I know this is an emotional time for you, Bobby. I can't think what you must be going through. Nia's condition—have the doctors said anything else?" (Johnson, 2003, p. 124).

Bobby looks around the room. He sees images of happy families posing with their children. He then looks back at the adoption papers:

> I look at the adoption papers stacked in front of me, then fold them in half before I tear them.
>
> "No, I don't know anything about raising a kid. I'm sixteen and none of those people on the wall look like the kind of family me and Feather's gonna be. But I'm doing it."
>
> The social worker's forehead wrinkles up.
>
> "You don't have to do it. This baby is wanted. There's a family that wants her. They're set up to take her and love her—"
>
> "But I love her, and even though I'm not set up for her, she's mine. And I'm hers."
>
> When I walk out of the office I think I see "Just Frank" standing at the end of the hall. And then I know I'm being a man, not just some kid who's upset and wants it his way.
>
> I'm being a man. (Johnson, 2003, pp. 124–125)

Bobby experiences an awakening of sorts in this moment. He can't explain why he must rip up the adoption papers and chart a path that neither he nor Nia ever considered. However, in that moment, he grasps the uncertainty as well as the assurance that keeping Feather is the right thing that he knows in his heart he must do. This triumphant experience is punctuated by the realization that he entered the social worker's office a boy, but he left a man. He is not acting like an impulsive, petulant teenager; rather, he zooms way out, no longer thinking of himself. He knows that his daughter needs him, and he needs her.

Embedded in this remarkable book about family, responsibility, and love is a story about life—the ups and downs and twists and turns that serve as illustrations of the journey we all embark on while trying to make meaning out of everything we experience. Bobby's story in *The First Part Last* captures the very essence of life, and while all readers won't know what it is like to raise a child, everyone will understand the heights of a triumph and the depths of a life-altering tragedy. Leveraging these kinds of stories when teaching writing is an excellent entry point for students to begin a more relevant and authentic writing experience.

INSTRUCTIONAL ACTIVITIES

Personal narrative writing hasn't always played a central role in secondary English/language arts classes, but it can become a transformational opportunity for students to not only develop as writers but also access their lived experiences in a way that allows for growth and maturity. The Triptych Narrative project (Sedun & Skillen, 2015) is one of many ways personal narrative writing can be used to develop these skills and to create these kinds of opportunities in the classroom.

The First Part Last can serve as a mentor text that students can draw from as they create their own narrative writing. Several examples will be provided in the following section, but it is important to note that the other novels discussed in this text can also serve as mentor texts for the Triptych Narrative project.

Triptych Narratives

The Triptych Narrative project invites students to write three stories—a tribute, a tragedy, and a triumph—using a variety of storytelling modes. Much like a triptych tells a story in three panels, the Triptych Narrative project tells a life story in three pieces of writing. In most common applications of this project, at least one piece is a narrative essay, and the others are presented in poetry, diary entries, drawings, paintings, collages, and the like. The full spectrum of storytelling is open for the storytellers to best illustrate their experience, their life story, in three pieces.

The Tribute

In our lived experiences, we have encountered those who have made a tremendous impact on our lives. So great is their impact that we cannot imagine who we would be without their guidance, love, and support. The first story that is often written in the Triptych Narrative project is a piece about someone who has given tirelessly and endlessly of themselves for us.

Writing this story is often quite approachable. Most students can think of at least one person close to them who is worthy of recognition. Writing teachers might encounter some tension when asking students to write about someone important to them if students pick pop culture heroes or professional athletes. Pushing back gently on these notions is an important step in the writing process. Asking, instead, for students to focus in on the people closer to them for this piece allows student writers to develop a part of their own life story while examining how someone else's life has overlapped with theirs.

In *The First Part Last*, there are several instances in which Bobby makes small tributes to his parents. As he has become a parent himself, he sees the work, the loyalty, and the heartbreak that comes with parenthood. There are also several great instances in which Bobby gives tribute to his daughter, Feather. One such example can be found in a "now" section:

Her eyes are the clearest eyes I've ever seen.
　　Sometimes she looks at me like she knows me. Like she's known me forever, and everything I ever thought, too. It's scary how she looks at me.
　　And she's so new. Been on the planet for only a few months. I been thinking about it a whole lot lately. I feel old. (Johnson, 2003, p. 80)

In this excerpt is a beautiful illustration of how two lives can intersect, overlap, and completely envelop one another. Through a single look, Bobby observes his daughter and sees a new perspective on life and the very essence of the connected human experience. She is so new, yet she sees right through him. This is the level of connectedness that can be revealed in our closest relationships, and these relationships are worth a tribute.

The Triumph

Overcoming great obstacles, standing up in the face of injustice, and speaking truth to power are all tremendously triumphant experiences, and it is these kinds of stories that often contrast the tragedies we experience. These stories, these triumphant successes, are the mountaintop experiences that we hope live well beyond our time on earth. They are the stories that define us.

Commonly, student writers will easily access periods of their lives in which they were triumphant—in the sports arena. No matter the age or ability of the student writer, it is often a good idea to offer more coaching. While victory in a game is certainly memorable, these experiences are not often unique. Instead, it might be a better idea to explore transitions in one's life when looking for a truly triumphant story to tell.

Just as Bobby comes to the remarkable realization that he is no longer a boy when he tears up the adoption papers and proclaims that *he* is Feather's father, students of all ages have encountered moments when they bravely faced a significant transition or change in their lives and came out of it better, stronger people. These are the triumphs that tell a person's story, and they are certainly worth sharing.

The Tragedy

Depending on the audience one is working with, the tragedy can either be the easiest or the most difficult piece to write. When working with personal tragedy, it is often best to share a number of mentor texts with students in which people their age deal with setbacks, challenges, and failure.

An excellent excerpt to talk about failure and disappointment in *The First Part Last* can be found in a "now" chapter starting on page 69. In this section, writing teachers can explore with their students how dialogue and emotional description can capture how a person might feel knowing he or she has made a mistake that has affected others. We've all been there, and Johnson, through Bobby's voice, describes how we might feel when we have a really big mess to clean up.

Moving from the mentor text to the students' writing might be a little difficult at first. A good technique to try is to use the mentor text as a model. The first line of this section of the text says, "I gotta catch a break." Inviting students to start their own writing with this line might be a way to help them find a story in which they really struggled or when they experienced setbacks.

The beauty of this project is seen when all three stories are presented together. Throughout the academic term or the instructional process, each piece will be developed as a stand-alone story, poem, picture, or production. But when they ultimately come together, when the writer can see the connective tissue that holds the stories together, this is when the triptych life story becomes a masterpiece in and of itself.

CONCLUSION

Bobby's story, as seen in the pieces and parts threaded expertly together in *The First Part Last*, is a story of tremendous tragedy and remarkable courage. It is touching, and it is truth. This is what personal narrative can reveal in the lives of all student writers, and it can transform every reader too.

SELECTED BIBLIOGRAPHY

Johnson, A. (1993). *Do like Kyla*. New York: Orchard Books.

Johnson, A. (1995). *Shoes like Miss Alice's*. New York: Orchard Books.

Johnson, A. (1998). *Heaven*. New York: Simon & Schuster.

Johnson, A. (2000). *Daddy calls me man*. New York: Orchard Books.

Johnson, A. (2000). *When mules flew on Magnolia Street*. New York: Alfred A. Knopf.

Johnson, A. (2003). *I dream of trains*. New York: Simon & Schuster.

Johnson, A. (2004). *Just like Josh Gibson*. New York: Simon & Schuster.

Johnson, A. (2007). *A sweet smell of roses*. New York: Simon & Schuster.

Johnson, A. (2007). *Lily Brown's paintings*. New York: Orchard Books.

Johnson, A. (2010). *Sweet, hereafter*. New York: Simon & Schuster.

Johnson, A. (2013). *A certain October*. New York: Simon & Schuster.

Johnson, A. (2014). *All different now: Juneteenth, the first day of freedom*. New York: Simon & Schuster.

REFERENCES

Johnson, A. (n.d.). Interview for Encyclopedia of Biographies. Retrieved from https://www.notablebiographies.com/news/Ge-La/Johnson-Angela.html#ixzz6CXqgR9ui.

Johnson, A. (2003). *The first part last*. New York: Simon & Schuster.

Johnson, A. (2009). Interview by Kelly Starling Lyons, February 8, 2009. Retrieved from https://thebrownbookshelf.com/28days/angela-johnson/.

Sedun, A., & Skillen, M. (2015). The breath of life: The power of narrative. *English Journal, 104*(5), 102–105.

Chapter 4

Nikki Grimes

Poet, Writer, Advocate, and Creative Spirit

Mary Napoli and Barbara A. Ward

One of the most versatile authors in children's and young adult publishing, noted poet Nikki Grimes has been writing books for children for much of her life. She first began her authorial career writing several Little Golden books and various trade books for Disney before receiving acclaim for her beloved picture book *Meet Danita Brown* in 1994. Writing was a refuge for Grimes, who grew up in Harlem. She began writing at the age of six, developing a keen appreciation for the stories told by others and crafting her own tales as well.

From picture books for children—including her most recent book, *Southwest Sunrise* (2020), which explores a boy's growing appreciation for his new desert home—to poetry collections to her Sibert Honor and Printz Honor memoir, *Ordinary Hazards* (2019), Grimes's deft touch with difficult topics has given wings to the stories and words she shares with her wide audience.

CRITICAL RECEPTION

Nikki Grimes's illustrious body of work and countless literary contributions have been celebrated and recognized with multiple honors. In 2017, the prolific poet and author received the Children's Literature Legacy Award from the American Library Association of Library Services to Children for her lifetime contribution as a poet and novelist as well as the 2016 Virginia Hamilton Literary Award.

These acknowledgments of her lengthy career and influence on literature for young readers should come as no surprise, since she's been writing in various formats and genres for several decades, starting with her novel

Growin' (1977) and picture book *Meet Danitra Brown* (1994). In 2006, she was the recipient of the National Council of Teachers of English Excellence in Poetry for Children Award for her body of work, and her writing has been recognized with multiple accolades and professional distinctions, including a Coretta Scott King Author Award for her groundbreaking verse novel *Bronx Masquerade* in 2003.

Teachers across the globe turn to that work and its companion, *Between the Lines* (2018), for poetic inspiration for their students and as evidence that poetry is relevant and meaningful and provides a space for self-expression and voice. Nikki Grimes is the author of more than thirty titles for children and adolescents and has written many articles and poems for popular trade journals. With the recent publication of her memoir, *Ordinary Hazards*, and poetry collection, including *Legacy: Women Poets of the Harlem Renaissance* (2021), Grimes shows no signs of slowing down, and her writing is just as relevant and descriptive as it has been from the onset.

CRITICAL DISCUSSION

In this empowering poetry collection, *One Last Word: Wisdom from the Harlem Renaissance*, Nikki Grimes masterfully juxtaposes original works from the Harlem Renaissance, penned by poets such as Langston Hughes, Countee Cullen, Georgia Douglas Johnson, and five others, alongside her own words. Not only does she include informative notes about the Harlem Renaissance and the poets whose words gave her "wings," but she uses their lines for creative inspiration.

In this volume of poetry, she crafts poems through the Golden Shovel poetic form, in which a poet borrows the words from a line or several lines of an existing poem and arranges them vertically in the right margin as the last word to create a new poem, essentially distilling the essence of the original poem. For example, a line from "As the Eagle Soars" by Jean Toomer ("Let your doing be an exercise, not an exhibition") inspires Nikki Grimes's "No Hamsters Here."

In Grimes's creative message of resilience in times of adversity, the anchor words (in bold font in the book) pay homage to the past and invite contemplation of contemporary issues: "Exercise / your unique talents to learn, grow, be your best—not / to prove anything to anyone, though that may well be an / added benefit! Life is an art, Son, not an exhibition."

One Last Word was initially well received upon its publication and then garnered numerous accolades in 2018, the year after it was published, including the Lee Bennett Hopkins Poetry Award (winner), Notable Books for a

Global Society, Boston Globe-Horn Book Award for Excellence in Children's Literature, and the Arnold Adoff Poetry Award for Middle Readers. The title was also lauded on several annual best-of lists and was named the New York Public Library Best Kids Book of the Year; *Kirkus Reviews* Best Book of the Year, Middle Grade; and *School Library Journal* Best Book of the Year, Nonfiction. Not only does *One Last Word* build on the works of innovative writers, but also Grimes transforms those original thoughts from several decades ago into new and powerful poems that will resonate with a new generation of writers and visionaries. Furthermore, the poetry collection features fifteen captivating and vibrant illustrations by well-known artists. Finally, the inspired collection of voices and themes also includes brief poet and artist biographies.

INSTRUCTIONAL ACTIVITIES

One Last Word provides a plethora of interdisciplinary opportunities for teachers to incorporate poems that inspire meaningful reflection. The poems provide connections to units of study pertaining to the Harlem Renaissance and offer an introduction to a lesser-known poetic form (the Golden Shovel) while showcasing the contemporary artwork of African American artists.

Because the poems from the Harlem Renaissance harken back to the early decades of the twentieth century, while the new ones written by Grimes explore similar themes and issues, the collection provides teachers and students with poetic contemplations of the struggles of the past and the challenges of the present. Blending the past with the present, readers will come to recognize the relevance of the words written several decades ago.

Teachers can provide students with opportunities to read, write, and engage in the richness of words while honoring the resilience of the human spirit through Grimes's sixteen poems and the ones that provided inspiration for them. Teachers can visit the poet's website (www.nikkigrimes.com) for instructional resources and explore the suggestions below for classroom engagements that support interdisciplinary connections.

Individual and Pair Share

Teachers can invite individual students to locate an inspirational poem or selection of writing as a springboard for creating an original Golden Shovel poem as described on pages 6–7 in *One Last Word*. Next, students can work with partners to explore the craft and structure of the poems and discuss their personal responses, feelings, and impressions. Through individual and small-group reading conferences, students will take notice of the imagery, tone, and style as well as each unique authorial voice, possibly even exploring the different word choices used by the poets.

If possible, teachers can collaborate with the fine arts teacher to expand on visual literacy and artistic appreciation to create a multimodal poetic response incorporating images as well as dance, musical, and/or dramatic responses. Students can create individual and original artistic responses to their poems using a variety of media and styles inspired by the illustrators of *One Last Word*. Students can also respond in Padlet or Nearpod to open-ended questions such as these:

- How do different art forms convey emotion?
- How do artists express what they think and feel?
- What can the arts teach us about the past?

Individually and with partners, students may recite their poems and showcase their artistic responses in a digital production (e.g., a short movie, a video, a podcast, or even an online graphic series; see textbox 4.1). Another possibility would be to invite students to explore approved images through Creative Commons to create a digital collage. Individually, students can also capture their interpretations of the poem by creating a Wordle or Tagxedo word cloud.

TEXTBOX 4.1   MULTIMODAL POETIC RESPONSE

A multimodal poetic response involves students writing, responding, and creating visual and oral responses to poetry. Because writing may change according to the intended audience, this activity affords students the chance to adapt their poetic and artistic responses according to different audiences, perhaps shortening or lengthening those responses as well as practicing dramatic readings of their pieces.

Keeping in mind that students must have access to literacy practices that guide their meaning making through multiple literacies, teachers can invite their whole class to respond to *One Last Word* by incorporating multimodal communication methods while developing multiliteracies through multigenre writing projects (Allen, 2001; Allen & Swistak, 2004; Romano, 2000).

Originally developed by Tom Romano, multigenre projects allow students to express themselves creatively through various modes while still demonstrating critical thinking and analysis, research, writing, and communication skills. Multigenre projects allow students to explore the text as a whole group and provide individual interpretations. Finally, by working in small groups or with partners, students can research writers, artists, and singers of the Harlem Renaissance using both print and digital resources.

In this capacity, students can carry out the role of investigator/researcher to explore questions such as these:

- How did the writers of the Harlem Renaissance shape the movement?
- How did the particular time and place in which these writers were working shape their work?

Students would then reflect on their findings to compose a multigenre project that demonstrates critical thinking, analysis, and creativity. (See textbox 4.2.)

TEXTBOX 4.2   HARLEM RENAISSANCE MULTIGENRE RESEARCH PROJECT

Mixing ingenuity, research, reading, and writing can turn the typical research paper assignment into an interesting and authentic process. Multigenre research projects allow students to create layers of meaning using various genres of response about a specific topic, such as the Harlem Renaissance.

As students explore the rich background of historical and cultural influences that shaped the artwork, music, and writing that was created during this period, they can structure their responses using various genres and formats.

Students may employ different writing modes (e.g., narrative, expository, persuasive) across different forms, such as poetry, song lyrics, pictures, narratives, dramatic or musical performances, video clips, blog posts, text messages, tweets, news articles, diary entries, and letters (Allen, 2001; Allen & Swistak, 2004; Romano, 2000). When their work is complete, students can participate in a writing celebration or a gallery walk to showcase their work.

Despite its importance, the period of the Harlem Renaissance has received little attention in history books or literature anthologies. By having student groups delve deeply into this period during the 1920s and 1930s, when Harlem attracted and nurtured many creative spirits, teachers can help students learn about the importance of a supportive community. Some students may even go so far as to find their own creative communities in their high school or town as they recognize the importance of a sense of place for artists, writers, and musicians.

Small-Group Instruction

Teachers can also support multiliteracies by inviting small groups of students to capture and share their developing voices by producing a poetry podcast. Teachers may wish to review the curriculum guide and helpful suggestions provided by National Public Radio (https://www.npr.org/2018/11/15/662070097 /starting-your-podcast-a-guide-for-students).

One avenue to guide students to become active constructors of their own knowledge is through the cocreation of a podcast. To begin, teachers invite their learners to critically reflect on and consider the structure of existing public podcasts, including one with Nikki Grimes available at http://www .allthewonders.com/podcasts/nikki-grimes-all-the-wonders-episode-347 (see textbox 4.3).

TEXTBOX 4.3   PODCASTS

Podcasts provide students with opportunities to build their speaking and listening skills while collaborating with their peers. Students can design a podcast featuring the work of one of the poets featured in *One Last Word* (Grimes, 2017).

Students can also access Listenwise (https://listenwise.com), a digital collection of podcasts and public radio broadcasts featuring a variety of topics. It is important for students to be able to explore how others have approached these creative tasks because this can build confidence for those who are reluctant to write creatively. When students are provided with a significant number of models or mentor texts, they are often more willing to take a risk and produce something beyond their original comfort zone.

As students embrace the possibility of creating a podcast, they will negotiate the content and digital tools, such as Audacity, GarageBand, or Podbean, needed in production. Before recording their podcast, students would prepare a sample script that imagines how the featured poets from *One Last Word* might respond to questions about their writing. These scripts can also be shared in small groups so that students can receive feedback from their peers and then edit to make the piece stronger.

Students could also read and dramatically interpret how the poems might have been performed. Since podcasts lend themselves to enhanced social learning, they provide a rich context in which speaking and listening skills can be extended and celebrated. Students could research each of the poets and then write individual poems about an issue that speaks to them, using the poetic style of their selected poet. Another extension might be to invite students to try their hands at writing one of their group members' poems using the Golden Shovel poetic form before recording their voices.

Whole-Class Instruction

In addition to whole-group poetry readings and discussions, teachers can also introduce key vocabulary, create anchor charts for writing, and model dramatic interpretation. For example, before students create an individual Golden Shovel poem, teachers will conduct several mini lessons about the poetic form. This is a method of introducing Grimes's *One Last Word* to the class before reading the book as a class or as individuals. Adding this information to the introduction not only awakens students to the poetry of the Harlem Renaissance but also helps students expand their understanding of different poetic forms and how they function.

For more inspiration, teachers can share examples from members of the Poetry Friday community found in poet Irene Latham's 2018 blog post "A Roundup of Golden Shovel Poems in Honor of Nikki Grimes's *One Last Word*" (https://irenelatham.blogspot.com/2018/02/a-roundup-of-golden-shovel-poems-in.html). Another option is to share the video of Nikki Grimes reading "Jabari Unmasked" to facilitate discussion (https://www.nikkigrimes.com/videos/videos_nikkis_jam.html).

Teachers can organize a multimodal text set including videos, transcripts, interviews, music, and other literature selections to read aloud and support learning. By incorporating music, poetry, and art related to the Harlem Renaissance, students can compare and contrast artistic elements while discussing their historical contexts. Teachers are encouraged to use paired texts such as *One Last Word* with *Harlem Stomp! A Cultural History of the Harlem Renaissance* (Hill, 2004) to compare and contrast Grimes's chosen words with those of others (see textbox 4.4).

TEXTBOX 4.4   MULTIMODAL TEXT SETS AND AUTHOR STUDIES

Multimodal text sets and author studies provide opportunities to deepen a shared understanding of material. Partnering both primary and secondary sources about the Harlem Renaissance has the capacity to build access to varied texts (e.g., audio, video, print, and visual) while promoting student engagement and conversation.

Middle-grade teachers may opt to co-plan lessons with social studies colleagues in order to facilitate interdisciplinary connections. Teachers can also incorporate suggestions available from the publisher (https://media.blooms bury.com/rep/files/OneLastWord_Guide.pdf). Finally, teachers could infuse Nikki Grimes's body of work within an author study.

One Last Word offers a plethora of instructional possibilities through multimodal poetic responses. After exploring the collection, teachers could invite students to locate a poem or piece of writing that prompts inspiration and create a Tagxedo or Wordle word cloud with initial impressions. Teachers might want to review the Golden Shovel poetic form on pages 6 and 7 of *One Last Word* and have students create an original poem or have the class members create one together after the teacher models how to do so.

Those who are more visually inclined might enjoy using a digital camera, digital images, or original art inspired by the different illustrative styles highlighted in the collection to respond to the student- or class-crafted poem or one of the selected poems in the Grimes text.

CONCLUSION

Naturally, the exploration of the poems in *One Last Word* may foster even more curiosity about the historical context of the Harlem Renaissance itself as well as a need to read more from Grimes. In addition, partly because Grimes is familiar to teen readers through her poetry and books for a younger audience, they are likely to trust her and willingly seek out her works, even when they are as challenging as *One Last Word*.

Some students may find inspiration in the author's versatility and choose to emulate the Golden Shovel poetic form, while others may decide to invent their own form. Ultimately, although her book might proclaim to offer "one last word" on the Harlem Renaissance and life's challenges, it serves as a conversation starter and reminder of resilience. As her last poem concludes with hope, "You and me, / we're going to be okay. / I know life will be rough, / but we've got the stuff / to make it" (Grimes, 2017, p. 94). It is hard to think of words more fitting for these trying times.

SELECTED BIBLIOGRAPHY (MIDDLE YOUNG ADULT)

Grimes, N. (1998). *Jazmin's notebook*. New York: Dial Books for Young Readers.
Grimes, N. (2002). *Bronx masquerade*. New York: Dial Books for Young Readers.
Grimes, N. (2005). *Dark sons*. New York: Jump at the Sun/Hyperion Books for Children.

Grimes, N. (2006). *Road to Paris*. New York: G. P. Putnam's Sons.

Grimes, N. (2011). *Planet middle school*. New York: Bloomsbury.

Grimes, N. (2013). *Words with wings*. Honesdale, PA: Wordsong.

Grimes, N. (2016). *Garvey's choice*. Honesdale, PA: Wordsong.

Grimes, N. (2017). *One last word: Wisdom from the Harlem Renaissance*. New York: Bloomsbury Children's Books.

Grimes, N. (2019). *Ordinary hazards*. Honesdale, PA: Wordsong.

Grimes, N. (2021). *Legacy: Women poets of the Harlem Renaissance*. New York: Bloomsbury Children's Books.

ADDITIONAL CHILDREN'S LITERATURE SELECTIONS

Grimes, N. (1994). *Meet Danitra Brown* (F. Cooper, Illus.). New York: HarperCollins.

Grimes, N. (2020). *Southwest sunrise* (W. Minor, Illus.). New York: Bloomsbury Children's Books.

Hill, L. C. (2004). *Harlem stomp! A cultural history of the Harlem Renaissance*. New York: Little, Brown and Company.

REFERENCES

Allen, C. (2001). *The multigenre research paper*. Portsmouth, NH: Heinemann.

Allen, C., & Swistak, L. (2004). Multigenre research: The power of choice and interpretation. *Language Arts, 81*(3), 223–232.

Grimes, N. (2017). *One last word: Wisdom from the Harlem Renaissance*. New York: Bloomsbury Children's Books.

Romano, T. (2000). *Blending genre, altering style: Writing multiple genre papers*. Portsmouth, NH: Heinemann.

Vardell, S. M., & Oxley, P. (2007). An interview with poet Nikki Grimes. *Language Arts, 84*(3), 281–285.

Yokota, J. (2017). To know Nikki Grimes is to know an artist. *Horn Book Magazine*, July/August, 38–41.

Chapter 5

Nikki Grimes

Poetry as Memoir

Mary Napoli and Barbara A. Ward

Nikki Grimes was one of the first authors of books for middle graders and teens to rely on the novel in verse format, a form that captures readers' attention quickly, provides immediacy into the story, and gives readers glimpses into the hearts and minds of characters. This trailblazing author has received much acclaim for her work, which includes picture books such as the timely *Kamala Harris: Rooted in Justice* (2020) and *Bedtime for Sweet Creatures* (2020). Her versatility and ability to capture universal human experiences make her books a popular choice for students, teachers, and librarians.

CRITICAL DISCUSSION

Known for her fiction and poetry, the author Nikki Grimes unearths a mother lode of treasure as she mines her life for the award-winning and heartfelt memoir *Ordinary Hazards* (2019). Relying on a series of poems with short titles, Grimes describes her formative years, sharing both the low points and challenges as well as the hopeful moments. This particular book holds the distinction of being named a Michael Printz Honor Book (Young Adult) and Robert F. Sibert Honor Book (Nonfiction) and receiving the 2020 Boston Globe–Horn Book Honor Award for Nonfiction and the Arnold Adoff Poetry Award for Teens.

 Ordinary Hazards features extraordinary lines from a remarkable poet who distills her memories of the "ordinary hazards" that she encountered during her tender years in honest, gut-wrenching fashion. Not only is this a memoir that honors one girl's resilience; it also demonstrates the power of literacy and faith in helping someone survive trauma and somehow remain intact with hope for the future. Grimes offers glimpses of a young girl's determination as she survives years of abuse and neglect and finds hope and possibility through reading and writing.

Grimes demonstrates that she is at the peak of her writing talent in this memoir, deftly describing her own emotional and physical abuse and her concerns about following in the footsteps of her mother with mental illness. The loneliness and uncertainty of being moved from one home or family to another and shuttling between neighborhoods are offset by her love of dance, music, and literature and the supportive individuals who kept her going and nurtured her dreams.

She deftly weaves together the book's sections, which are separated into different time periods, with Book One covering the years of 1950 to 1955, Book Two covering 1955 to 1960, Book Three covering 1960 to 1963, and Book Four covering 1964 to 1966. Each section contains original poems as well as sections entitled "Notebook" interspersed between the poems. The "Notebook" entries are based on the author's memories and imaginings of what she recorded in her own notebook at the time. This device is necessary since her original notebooks were destroyed by her mother.

Many students may be reluctant to try to write anything about their early years, since they most likely were not keeping a journal of any kind at that time and may feel intimidated at the thought of writing honestly and accurately. But as Grimes points out in her author's note, writing a memoir is challenging because it tries to arrive at truth, and truth and facts may not be the same.

This distinction is similar to what academics delving into research encounter when they realize there is no capital T Truth but rather many types of truth. While there is one universal truth when it comes to some types of research, such as medical research, that is not the case with qualitative studies, which seek to find multiple answers and interpretations for questions. So it is with memory, as one person's recollection of an event may be very different from another's due to perspective or focus. The ever-shifting sands of time may blur certain events while bringing others into sharper focus. Students might have experienced this when trying to determine if something is a memory of an event or an image recalled from looking at photographs in a well-thumbed family album.

Some of Grimes's pieces in *Ordinary Hazards* offer glimpses into the historical events through which she was living. No ordinary memoir, *Ordinary Hazards* shines a light on one way to survive, providing a lifeline for those who may have experienced hazards similar to Grimes's. Many readers will see themselves in this woman's story while also recognizing possible ways to navigate through their own life challenges.

INSTRUCTIONAL ACTIVITIES

This book not only charts the course of one writer's budding career but also serves as an excellent example of memoir writing for English language arts classrooms. Writing a memoir has the potential to engage students in personal, meaningful writing activities, since they are writing about their own lives rather than responding to artificial prompts provided by teachers. This type of writing can be therapeutic, meaningful, and empowering.

Because so many students approach writing with great trepidation, it can be freeing for them to read about how even published writers found the writing process somewhat mysterious at first before finally coming to value it. As an example, teachers may share lines such as these found in "Secret" to prompt students to consider the power of writing to save and to heal: "This writing thing / was some kind of magic trick / I didn't yet understand" (Grimes, 2019, p. 60). They could also highlight these lines from "Journey" that mark the beginning of this poet's love affair with writing: "My life in notebooks / began with this, / a poem here, / an observation there. . . . The daily march of words / parading from my pen / kept me moving forward" (Grimes, 2019, p. 61).

Many will draw sustenance from Grimes's means of coping with being the new girl in yet another school, having moved yet again in the middle of the term. In "New Girl" she writes that "surviving is almost easy / if you have a strategy / and a copy of *A Wrinkle in Time*" (Grimes, 2019, p. 223). Getting lost in books and the library, where Grimes spent lonely lunch hours with her literary companions, also allowed her to study the craft of writing and learn from the masters.

Teachers could have students read Grimes's "The Mystery of Memory #1," "The Mystery of Memory #2," "The Mystery of Memory #3," and "The Mystery of Memory #4," and discuss the mystery of memories in their own lives, as well as the specific memories Grimes shares here. Subsequently, they may benefit by dividing their own memoir into various time periods or experiences.

Several websites provide prompts to help budding memoirists, including Authority Pub, which offers sixty-three memoir prompts (https://authority. pub/memoir-writing-prompts). Students may find it beneficial to explore such questions as these:

- What is your happiest memory from your childhood?
- What is your saddest memory from your childhood?
- What words did your parents use most often when you were a child?

Another helpful writing website, GoTeenWriters, named to *Writer's Digest*'s list "101 Best Websites for Writers" (https://goteenwriters.com), offers tips and examples of how to begin and end pieces as well as tackling hard topics such as those covered in *Ordinary Hazards*.

Plumbing one's earliest memories or examining relationships, books, or experiences that were important in one's childhood can be useful starting places for memoir writing.

Before Reading

Given the subject matter covered in *Ordinary Hazards*, the book offers the perfect opportunity for students to learn more about childhood trauma, mental health resources, and triggering experiences. Individually and in small groups, students can complete inquiry projects related to mental health.

Before students read *Ordinary Hazards*, teachers may want to show clips from the documentary *Paper Tigers* (2015) about the teachers, administrators, and students in Lincoln High School in Walla Walla, Washington, or view the trailer (http://papertigersmovie.com). This film traces how adolescents who have experienced challenging childhood experiences find ways to cope with help from their teachers and support systems.

Students might want to explore adverse childhood experiences at the Centers for Disease Control and Prevention's website (https://www.cdc .gov/violenceprevention/aces/index.html) or check out a questionnaire found on the Knowledge Works website (https://knowledgeworks.org/resources/ace -assessment-how-used/). Finally, teachers can invite local mental health professionals and community groups to visit the class to share resources.

During Reading

As students reflect on the novel independently and in small or whole groups, teachers can weave in various literacy engagements to support comprehension during reading. In addition to having students maintain a reader response journal to capture written reflections, teachers can include arts-based connections such as drama, music, visual arts, and photography.

Connection to the Arts

Drama provides students with the opportunity to interpret their personal experiences and express their feelings. By dramatizing a scene from their memoir, students will provide their peers with a better understanding of their challenges and life story. Alternatively, students can use the tableau drama strategy to encourage others to think more deeply about their memoir. The tableau drama strategy invites students to freeze in poses to create a picture of an important moment in a play.

Teachers can adapt this strategy to invite students to reflect on their individual life story and focus on one significant moment. Students will then express this moment in a series of poses and facial expressions. (See textbox 5.1.)

TEXTBOX 5.1   INFUSING THE ARTS IN CLASSROOMS THROUGH WRITING

Infusing the arts within the writing classroom supports rich meaning-making connections. Using drama, music, and visual arts to express human emotions and personal memories guides students to recognize commonalities while celebrating individual reflection and growth.

Music

Music is universal and provides moments of joy, healing, and understanding. Students can work individually or in small groups to explore song lyrics that align with the most significant parts of their lives. Inviting students to create a personal life story playlist or soundtrack is an excellent way to honor their stories while building an affinity with their peers. Teachers are encouraged to share with students their own personal playlist aligned to a personal memory or significant events.

Teachers may wish to read Chris Goering's (2004) article in which he describes his Soundtrack of Your Life assignment, which has been effectively incorporated in many classrooms. Alternatively, students can explore different song titles for the individual sections of *Ordinary Hazards*. They could work independently or in small groups to explore connections to music and link their discussion to overarching literary devices (e.g., mood, symbolism, imagery).

Visual Arts and Photography

As students stop to reflect on the different chapters, they can use a myriad of art supplies to express their emotions. Students can also opt to use photographs or digital images to spark discussion, reflection, and creativity. Students can take photographs of nature or other encounters with everyday activity to reflect on their emotions. Teachers may wish to read Ralph Fletcher's

(2019) professional resource entitled "Focus Lessons: How Photography Enhances the Teaching of Writing" for more ways to spark students' creativity.

After Reading

In small discussion and work groups, students can select from one of the following young adult memoirs (see textbox 5.2) and record notes using digital tools. Students will not only discuss the major themes of the novel but also compare and contrast *Ordinary Hazards* and their chosen book. Over the last decade, a host of young adult memoirs have been published. A resourceful teacher can find many more, but these represent a quality sampling.

TEXTBOX 5.2   YOUNG ADULT MEMOIRS

Teachers can select a memoir from this list for their additional memoir activity:

Jacqueline Woodson, *Brown Girl Dreaming* (2016)
Tara Westover, *Educated* (2018)
Sharon Robinson, *Child of the Dream: A Memoir of 1963* (2019)
Laurie Halse Anderson, *Shout* (2019)
Jarrett J. Krosoczka, *Hey, Kiddo* (2018)
Jack Gantos, *Hole in My Life* (2002)
TaNehisi Coates, *Between the World and Me* (2015)
Trevor Noah, *Born a Crime* (2016)
Katie Rain-Hill, *Rethinking Normal: A Memoir in Transition* (2014)
George Takei, *They Called Us Enemy* (2019)
Bishakh Som, *Spellbound: A Graphic Memoir* (2020)

After students read published previews of the books listed above and have signed up for discussion groups, they will meet each day to share golden lines or favorite passages from the books. It is helpful for students to determine a reading schedule that fits in with the rest of the plans the teacher has for the class. Teachers might also review many of the resources describing literature circle activities available online or through the work of Harvey "Smokey" Daniels.

As a culminating activity, students will create a group poster, reader's theater, or book trailer that distills the essence of the book and advertises it to their classmates. Students could also use Flipgrid to record videos of their favorite passages and comment on their classmates' work. For further inspiration, students can listen to Nikki Grimes's 2020 Boston Globe–Horn Book Award for Nonfiction award acceptance speech at https://www.youtube.com /watch?v=TyU2U2Lpie4.

Studying Craft and Writing Process

Using the exemplar memoirs, students can study their craft and structure to begin an individual memoir writing project. Teachers will invite students to brainstorm significant topics from their lives. As students proceed through the writing process, they will have ample opportunity to participate in both individual and peer conferences as they publish their memoir using digital storytelling tools, such as Storybird or Little Bird Tales. Alternatively, students can compose a six-word memoir poem based on their lives.

Students can create found poems or blackout poems from one of their favorite pages or poems in *Ordinary Hazards*. In addition, students may want to craft their own "Where I'm From" poems following the template used by its originator. George Ella Lyon's poem "Where I'm From" has wide appeal for student writers, whether they were born on a farm or in a bustling urban area, since the lines are personal and draw on students' early experiences.

By inserting the names of their parents or their memories in such a minimalist format, writers realize that the words they have chosen are extremely specific and yet general enough to leave readers curious about the stories behind those words or phrases. Students can also opt to add photographs or images to enhance the overall aesthetic of the text.

After Reading

Teachers might want to invite students to compose their own multigenre memoir or create a video of an important moment in their life and include music, dance, poems, images, or art. Alternatively, students can work on a memoir video project where they prepare a video using WeVideo (https:// www.wevideo.com/education-resources) or Animoto (https://animoto.com). They would record their voices and include photographs, poems, and whatever other artifacts they feel represent their memory. To facilitate the recording process, students would complete a video story planner.

Students would also discuss the process of storytelling and complete a prewriting organizer using a storyboard. Students would review how telling a personal story using media is different from creating a written version. They can also analyze video examples to determine what makes them effective (e.g., logical movement, storyline) before planning their video memoir. Students can add approved background music, images, or sounds available through Creative Commons

There are many variations to support a memoir video project, including creating a six-word memoir video as described in textbox 5.3. This idea could be adapted from the beginning of the year to post readings of Grimes's work. Students could work independently on this video project and obtain peer feedback before presenting their work to the entire class.

TEXTBOX 5.3   SIX-WORD MEMOIR VIDEO PROJECT

To begin, check out the article "Breaking the Ice with Student-Made Videos" (https://www.edutopia.org/article/breaking-ice-student-made-videos). Students can respond to their six-word memoir poem by using digital tools to enhance and extend the overall personal significance of their memory. Finally, for additional suggestions, teachers may wish to review some of the ideas provided by the publisher in the article *"Ordinary Hazards: A Memoir*: A Discussion Guide with Common Core State Standard Correlations" (https://boydsmillsandkane.com/wp-content/uploads/2019/09/ORDINARY-HAZARDS-READERS-GUIDE-FEB-7.pdf).

While this assignment focuses on a video assignment, it can be modified to be presented through a poster or PowerPoint presentation. In our digital age, it is important that students have experience developing products within digital spaces. Helping them master digital tools will prepare them for future jobs.

CONCLUSION

Nikki Grimes remains one of the most important poets in America, not just within the world of Black poets and young adult poets. Her extraordinary memoir is a reminder of the breadth and depth of her work. Memoirs can be an important genre for adolescents to study. Memoirs remind them that all lives are important, even adolescent lives that are difficult and full of challenges. *Ordinary Hazards* demonstrates that adolescents can grow up to be adults who achieve wonderful things.

CHILDREN'S LITERATURE SELECTIONS

Anderson, L. H. (2019). *Shout*. New York: Viking Books for Young Readers.
Coates, T. (2015). *Between the world and me*. New York: One World/Penguin/Random House.

Gantos, J. (2002). *Hole in my life*. New York: Farrar, Straus, and Giroux.

Grimes, N. (2019). *Ordinary hazards*. Honesdale, PA: Wordsong.

Grimes, N. (2020). *Bedtime for sweet creatures* (E. Zunon, Illus.). Naperville, IL: Sourcebooks Jabberwocky.

Grimes, N. (2020). *Kamala Harris: Rooted in justice* (L. Freeman, Illus.). New York: Atheneum.

Krosoczka, J. J. (2018). *Hey, kiddo*. New York: Graphix.

Noah, T. (2016). *Born a crime*. New York: One World/Penguin/Random House.

Rain-Hill, K. (2014). *Rethinking normal: A memoir in transition*. New York: Simon & Schuster Books for Young Readers.

Robinson, S. (2019). *Child of the dream: A memoir of 1963*. New York: Scholastic.

Som, B. (2020). *Spellbound: A graphic memoir*. Brooklyn, NY: Street Noise Books.

Takei, G., Eisinger, J., & Scott, S. (2019). *They called us enemy* (H. Becker, Illus.). Marietta, GA: Top Shelf Productions.

Westover, T. (2018). *Educated: A memoir*. New York: Random House.

Woodson, J. (2014). *Brown girl dreaming*. New York: Nancy Paulsen Books.

REFERENCES

Fletcher, R. (2019). *Focus lessons: How photography enhances the teaching of writing.* Portsmouth, NH: Heinemann.

Goering, C. (2004). Music and the personal narrative: The dual track to meaningful writing. *The NWP [National Writing Project] Quarterly*, *26*(4). Retrieved from https://archive.nwp.org/cs/public/print/resource/2142.

Grimes, N. (2019). *Ordinary hazards*. Honesdale, PA: Wordsong.

Chapter 6

Constructing Understanding through Advocacy

A Critical Disability Studies Perspective on Sharon Draper's Out of My Mind

Kathryn Caprino and Tara Anderson Gold

The author of over thirty books, Sharon M. Draper is one of today's most popular and widely read authors for young adults. A former teacher, Draper now writes and visits with teachers and young adults throughout the world. Draper's works cover a variety of genres, including contemporary fiction, historical fiction, mystery, nonfiction, and poetry. This chapter will share Draper's critical reception, consider *Out of My Mind* in the context of critical disability studies (Goodley, 2013), and provide lesson activities informed by a critical literacy approach (Lewison, Flint, & Sluys, 2002).

CRITICAL RECEPTION

Draper's first novel, *Tears of a Tiger* (Draper, 1994), was written to be a fast-paced, high-interest book that could also be taught in the classroom (Peck & Hendershot, 1999). It landed on the American Library Association's Best Books for Young Adults list in 1995 and was also the first Draper novel to win a Coretta Scott King Literary Award from the American Library Association. Coretta Scott King Awards are given to African American authors and illustrators for outstanding stories representing "appreciation of African American culture and universal human values" (American Library Association, 2009).

In 2011, Draper was awarded the Lifetime Achievement Award for contributions to the field of adolescent literature by the Assembly on Literature for Adolescents of the National Council of Teachers of English. She won the prestigious Margaret A. Edwards Award for lifetime literary achievement from the American Library Association in 2015.

CRITICAL DISCUSSION

Out of My Mind (Draper, 2010) is the story of Melody, a bright eleven-year-old with spastic bilateral quadriplegia, also known as cerebral palsy. Melody has always lived in a world rich with words, even though she cannot speak. With the help of a new assistive technology called the Medi-Talker, she expresses her ideas. The novel explores Melody's journey of joining an inclusion class at her school, making friends, and participating in the school's Whiz Kids quiz competition. Along the way, she must work with people who champion her and those who treat her differently due to her differences.

In the novel's end note, Draper explains that Melody was inspired by her experience as a parent raising a child with developmental difficulties. Melody is not directly based on her daughter but is a "tribute to all the parents of [kids with disabilities] who struggle, to all those children who are misunderstood, to all those caregivers who help every step of the way" (Draper, "Behind the Book," 2010). Draper is clear that she wants Melody to be understood and loved as a person for whom disability is just one element of her character.

CRITICAL DISABILITY STUDIES AND *OUT OF MY MIND*

Perhaps departing from many other titles in Draper's oeuvre or other novels discussed in this book series, *Out of My Mind* is not about a person of color. When asked about the lack of racial identifiers in the text, Draper shared, "Her race is not important. Melody's difficulties far supersede any racial or cultural problems she might encounter" (Draper, "Intro, Summary, and General Questions," 2016). *Out of My Mind* can be examined through the lens of critical disability studies (Goodley, 2013).

Critical disability studies challenges understandings of disability as impairment, offering an understanding of disability as a complex interplay between both medical and social systems. This lens is used to question the binary oppositions of categories such as ability/disability, normal/abnormal, and even the medical model/social model altogether. In this view, people are actively disabled by the language, physical spaces, and social landscapes of a society that fails to account for diverse bodies.

Looking at Melody's story through the critical disability studies lens, readers can see that her disability is one defined by those around her: doctors, teachers, parents, and peers. Many of the people in Melody's life misunderstand or misdiagnose her impairments. When Melody is five, she is taken to a doctor who proclaims, "[It] is my opinion that Melody is severely brain-damaged and profoundly retarded" (Draper, 2010, p. 22). Her third-grade teacher continues teaching her the letters of the alphabet. And when Melody begins using her Medi-Talker at school, one of her classmates exclaims, "[It] just never occurred to me that Melody had thoughts in her head" (Draper, 2010, p. 143).

Melody's disability through the first half of the novel is constructed for her by those in her social world. She can think and understand the world around her but is unable to communicate her thoughts with anyone. Because of this impairment, others assume she has other impairments. She is placed in a special education class, where she is forced to review similar concepts each year. However, once Melody is able to communicate using the Medi-Talker, her peers, parents, and teachers realize that she thinks and processes just like others.

Melody has a near-photographic memory and earns the highest score on the qualifying test for the Whiz Kids quiz competition. The scene in which she tells a knock-knock joke allows students to see she has a sense of humor. The Medi-Talker makes it possible for those around her to understand that about her. This scene in particular illuminates the reality that Melody's story centers on a clear and literal social reclassification of her disability.

The first-person narration in the novel helps readers experience Melody's frustrations. In one instance, Melody sees toy blocks in the aisle at the store and has one of her "tornado explosions." Her mother thinks Melody is upset because she wants to play with the blocks, but Melody narrates that she saw on the news that the blocks had been recalled for containing lead paint. Readers can relate to the frustration of not being heard, understood, or able to express themselves.

Out of My Mind shows readers that disability is not necessarily a fixed medical diagnosis but rather a complex combination of factors. At first, the students in her new fifth-grade inclusion class struggle with how to socially connect with Melody. She watches them playing at recess and wishes they would talk to her, even if she cannot run and play tag with them. She also expresses frustration at how fast her teammates talk during quiz team practice and how she cannot type quickly enough to participate. These are experiences that many young people have never thought about but that make a huge impact on Melody's world.

The climax to this conflict comes when Melody is left behind by her team as they travel to the national quiz competition in Washington, DC. Melody is hurt when her teammates coordinate a last-minute earlier flight to miss an impending snowstorm without thinking of her. She advocates for herself by confronting her teammates. They feel bad; some cry, and some try to make amends with Melody. The story ends here, leaving readers unsure of what happens next. But the message is clear: Melody's teammates should have reached out to her.

Thinking from a critical disability studies perspective, readers can see that Melody's classmates (and teachers) often actively deny her the ability to speak, contribute, and participate, perpetuating her status as an outsider. However, they have the power and the responsibility to actively include her in their school community. Draper's (2010) end note to the novel explains that the story was written for "people who look away, who pretend they don't see, or who don't know what to say when they encounter someone who faces life with obvious differences" (n.p.).

INSTRUCTIONAL ACTIVITIES

To complement or extend the activities suggested at the end of the text (Draper, "Reading Group Guide," 2010) and on Sharon Draper's author website (Draper, "Study Guides," 2016), the three activities discussed below will help move students toward deeper understandings of the novel and toward taking steps to include those experiencing differences.

Framed by Lewison et al.'s (2002) work, these lessons move from individual to small-group to whole-class exercises. Lewison et al. (2002, p. 382) provide four critical literacy dimensions: "(1) disrupting the commonplace, (2) interrogating multiple viewpoints, (3) focusing on sociopolitical issues, and (4) taking action and promoting social justice."

Individual Activity: Moving toward Understanding through Synesthetic Poetry

The first activity is an individual writing exercise that invites students to write synesthetic poetry about their feelings as they move toward a deeper understanding of the distinction between feeling sorry for someone and understanding someone. Aligned with National Council of Teachers of English/International Reading Association (2012) Standard 12, "Students use spoken, written, and visual language to accomplish their own purposes (e.g., for learning, enjoyment, persuasion, and the exchange of information)," this lesson is motivated by Draper's (2010) end note in which she writes about how she wanted readers to interpret Melody and for whom *Out of My Mind* was written: "I was fiercely adamant that nobody feel sorry for Melody. I wanted her to be accepted as a character and as a person, not as a representative for people with disabilities. Melody is a tribute to all of the parents of disabled kids who struggle, to all those children who are misunderstood, to all those caregivers who help every step of the way" (Draper, "Behind the Book," 2010).

Students should first write a few lines of poetry in which they share how they felt when they wanted a person or group of people to understand them rather than feel sorry for them. Next, students should write a few lines of poetry in which they share how they felt when they did not try to understand a person but rather felt sorry for him or her or treated him or her in a way that was not right.

Encourage students to build on the text's use of synesthesia, defined as "a sensation produced in one modality when a stimulus is applied to another modality, as when the hearing of a certain sound induces the visualization of a certain color" ("Synesthesia," 2018), like Melody does here: "Country [music] is lemons—not sour, but sugar sweet and tangy. Lemon cake icing, cool, fresh lemonade!" (Draper, 2010, p. 6) or here: "I hear no beautiful colors" (p. 258).

Finally, teachers can ask these questions to help students reflect on their poems:

- How does understanding someone differ from feeling sorry for someone?
- How does reflecting on our own experiences help us understand Melody?
- How might reading *Out of My Mind* help us when we encounter a classmate who needs to be understood?

As they consider all students, not just students with disabilities, students will be engaging here with the "disrupting the commonplace" and "interrogating multiple viewpoints" components of Lewison et al.'s (2002, p. 382) work.

Small-Group Activity: "In Real Words," a Two-Part Lesson, Technological Focus

Technology is a crucial element of *Out of My Mind*. Whereas there are instances when Melody wishes she could communicate like the other kids, her Medi-Talker is what enables her to communicate more easily with her family and classmates. This small-group activity provides opportunities for students to consider the limitations and affordances of technological communication in the text and in their lives.

Technology's Limitations

When Melody receives her Medi-Talker, she is overjoyed. She adds many words to the computer, and one of the book's grand moments occurs when

Melody is able to tell her parents she loves them: "So I push a couple of buttons, and the machine speaks the words I've never been able to say. 'I love you'" (Draper, 2010, p. 138). Here, Melody and her parents experience something they have never experienced before: Melody's ability to tell her parents she loves them. Illustrated here and in other instances in *Out of My Mind*, Melody's situation is improved because of technology.

Technology has the ability to provide agency for adolescents who have mental or physical differences (Caprino & Gold, 2018). Yet, there are several instances in which Melody expresses that she is not always able to communicate in the manner she would like. For example, she states, "I want to be able to use the system to talk like ordinary kids. Sort of" (Draper, 2010, p. 137). She also states, "Just once I wish I could hug my little sister or tell my dad I love him too. In real words, not through a machine" (Draper, 2010, p. 242). Here, readers are able to see the limitations of Melody's computer.

Research supports that many teenagers are using social media in fantastic numbers (Lenhart, 2015). The first part of this lesson requires students to create data based on their social media communication and to analyze and discuss this data so they can think about the way their technologies, specifically digital devices, both aid and disrupt their ability to communicate. Students will create two columns. In the first column, they will write or type out the transcript of a recent text conversation they feel comfortable sharing with their classmates. Students who do not feel comfortable can compose a fictitious conversation. This transcript can be relatively short, approximately fifty words.

The second step invites students to type out how the conversation might have gone if it had happened face-to-face. Again, this transcript can be short but might be a bit longer than the first transcript, perhaps between one hundred and two hundred words. Students should then reflect individually, thinking about what they noticed while analyzing these two transcripts and the limitations and affordances of communicating in these different modes.

After students reflect individually, teachers will form small groups. In their groups, students will share their two transcripts and discuss how the conversations were different based on the modes. Students can discuss advantages and disadvantages of each mode before having conversations about Melody's situation. The following questions might guide students' discussions:

- In what ways does the analysis of our text and face-to-face communication relate to Melody's situation?
- How does Melody's technology enhance her communication?
- In what ways is Melody's communication still difficult despite her technology?

Technology's Affordances

The second part of this activity asks students to analyze their social media communication (e.g., text messages, Snapchat posts, Facebook posts) and think about what communication style (e.g., image, words) it privileges. For example, a social media post that includes a video of parents singing "Happy Birthday" to their son might be difficult to understand for someone who is hard of hearing or deaf. However, this same post with subtitles allows people who are hard of hearing or deaf to understand the post better. Similarly, those who add captions to their social media posts are enhancing the reading experiences of blind people who have technologies that will read the captions to them. Certainly, these are examples of technology's affordances. To extend the activity, teachers might ask students to think of other examples.

The first step in this part of the activity is for teachers to ask students to analyze their own social media posts. Students might pick a recent post in order to focus on the post's accessibility. They might discuss what elements of the post might make it challenging for a particular person by reflecting on the following questions: Can those with hearing difficulties understand the post? Can those who have vision challenges understand the post?

Answering these questions will move students toward the last step in this second part: reposting a social media post using two modes of communication. For example, students might add a caption to a recent picture they posted. Students might enjoy reviewing two resources as they revise their social media posts: Smith's (n.d.) poster "Golden Rules of Social Media Accessibility" (http://www.danya.com/files/sma_poster.pdf) and the University of Minnesota's (2018) "Accessible U" website (https://accessibility.umn.edu/tutorials/accessible-social-media).

As they critically analyze their social media accounts, students will be meeting National Council of Teachers of English/International Reading Association (2012) Standard 11: "Students participate as knowledgeable, reflective, creative, and critical members of a variety of literacy communities." Analyzing technology's limitations and affordances will help students become more critical about their technology use; encourage them to think about others' needs, thereby "interrogating multiple viewpoints" (Lewison et al., 2002, p. 382); and prepare them for our final activity: engaging in advocacy work.

Whole-Class Activity: Student Advocacy for Classmates

Our third teaching activity, a whole-class activity, involves student advocacy. As many recent student protests have exhibited, youths are capable of taking action to have their voices heard and to effect change. With the ultimate goal of improving the lives of those who need to be better understood, this activity requires students to work together as a class and design an advocacy project. This takes students back to one of Draper's goals for *Out of My Mind*: to understand better "all those children who are misunderstood" (Draper, "Behind the Book," 2010).

After engaging in the first two teaching activities and discussing Melody as a character and symbol for their classmates (or themselves) who might be misunderstood, teachers and students can engage in a multiweek, multi-disciplinary project in which they research a challenge a particular group of classmates or same-aged students within the community is having, design a solution, and put the solution into practice.

The challenges students take on need not be related specifically to classmates with cerebral palsy but should relate to improving classmates' or community members' lives. As they do this, students are meeting National Council of Teachers of English/International Reading Association (2012) Standard 7: "Students conduct research on issues and interests by generating ideas and questions, and by posing problems."

This activity will look different depending on class and school contexts and could result in students planning a collaborative activity between two groups of students (e.g., different grade levels), designing an assembly or field trip that helps classmates learn about how to include those who are misunderstood, creating literature or signage that might encourage classmates to be more accepting of others, or urging school leaders to change systems or policies that make school challenging for a particular student or group of students.

This lesson idea can engage students in "sociopolitical issues" (Lewison et al., 2002) in their lives or the lives of their classmates while moving them toward "taking action and promoting social justice" (p. 382). Using their reading of *Out of My Mind* as a catalyst to improve others' lives, students have the grand potential to advocate for greater acceptance of those who are misunderstood.

CONCLUSION

One of her many successful books, Draper's *Out of My Mind* is a true testament to a book's ability to evoke empathy and to urge understanding. Using the lens of critical disability studies to explore Melody's story in *Out of My Mind* provides meaningful opportunities for students to reflect and construct understanding through advocacy.

SELECTED BIBLIOGRAPHY

Draper, S. (1999). *Romiette and Julio*. New York: Atheneum.
Draper, S. (2001). *Double dutch*. New York: Atheneum.
Draper, S. (2006). *Copper sun*. New York: Atheneum.
Draper, S. (2013). *Panic*. New York: Atheneum.
Draper, S. (2015). *Stella by starlight*. New York: Atheneum.
Draper, S. (2018). *Blended*. New York: Atheneum.

The Jericho Trilogy

Draper, S. (2003). *The battle of Jericho*. New York: Atheneum.
Draper, S. (2007). *November blues*. New York: Atheneum.
Draper, S. (2009). *Just another hero*. New York: Atheneum.

The Hazelwood Trilogy

Draper, S. (1994). *Tears of a tiger*. New York: Atheneum.
Draper, S. (1997). *Forged by fire*. New York: Atheneum.
Draper, S. (2001). *Darkness before dawn*. New York: Atheneum.

SCHOLARLY WORKS TO BE CONSULTED

Bishop, R. S. (1990). Mirrors, windows, and sliding glass doors. *Perspectives*, *6*(3), ix–xi.
Curwood, J. S. (2013). Redefining normal: A critical analysis of (dis)ability in children's literature. *Children's Literature in Education*, *44*(1), 15–28.
Hughes, C. (2017). The "words inside": "Disabled" voices in contemporary literature for young people. *Journal of Literary and Cultural Disability Studies*, *11*(2), 187–203.
Shakespeare, T. (2006). The social model of disability. In L. Davis (Ed.), *The disability studies reader* (pp. 197–204). New York: Routledge.
Wheeler, E. A. (2013). No monsters in this fairy tale: *Wonder* and the new children's literature. *Children's Literature Association Quarterly*, *38*(3), 335–350.

REFERENCES

American Library Association. (2009). The history of the Coretta Scott King Book Awards. Retrieved from http://www.ala.org/rt/emiert/cskbookawards/about.
Caprino, K., & Gold, T. A. (2018). Examining agency in contemporary young adult illness narratives. *ALAN Review*.

Draper, S. (1994). *Tears of a tiger*. New York: Atheneum.

Draper, S. (2010). Behind the book. In *Out of my mind*. New York: Atheneum.

Draper, S. (2010). *Out of my mind*. New York: Atheneum.

Draper. S. (2016). Out of my mind intro, summary and general questions. Retrieved from http://sharondraper.com/bookdetail.asp?id=35.

Draper. S. (2016). Study guides. Retrieved from http://sharondraper.com/bookdetail.asp?id=35.

Goodley, D. (2013). Dis/entangling critical disability studies. *Disability and Society, 28*(5), 631–644.

Lenhart, A. (2015). Teens, social media and technology overview 2015. Retrieved from http://www.pewinternet.org/2015/04/09/teens-social-media-technology-2015/.

Lewison, M., Flint, A. S., & Sluys, K. V. (2002). Taking on critical literacy: The journey of newcomers and novices. *Language Arts, 79*(5), 382–392.

National Council of Teachers of English/International Reading Association. (2012). NCTE/IRA Standards for the English Language Arts. Retrieved from http://www.ncte.org/standards/ncte-ira.

Peck, J., & Hendershot, J. (1999). A conversation with Sharon M. Draper, winner of the 1998 Corretta Scott King Award. *Reading Teacher, 52*(7), 748–750.

Reading Group Guide. (2010). In *Out of my mind*. New York: Atheneum.

Smith, J. (n.d.). Golden rules of social media accessibility. Retrieved from http://www.danya.com/files/sma_poster.pdf.

Synesthesia (Def. 1). In Dictionary.com online. Retrieved from http://www.dictionary.com/browse/synesthesia?s=t.

University of Minnesota. (2018). Accessible social media. Retrieved from https://accessibility.umn.edu/tutorials/accessible-social-media.

Chapter 7

History, Memory, and Family Stories in Sharon Draper's *Stella by Starlight*

Morgan Jackson and Steven T. Bickmore

Draper is the perfect writer for teachers struggling to turn their students into readers. She was a teacher in Ohio for many years and turned to writing not only to fulfill her own goals but also to contribute books that offered mirrors, windows, and sliding glass doors for her students (Bishop, 1990). During the last twenty-five years, she has published a range of quality literature, won the prestigious Milken Educator Award (1997), was the 1997 National Teacher of the Year, and served as a literary ambassador representing the United States at a world book festival in Russia. Amid these accomplishments, her focus remains on the students who will read her books.

In chapter 6 of this volume, Caprino and Gold outline the breadth of Draper's range. It is important to note that Draper has not flinched from covering how issues of race have played out in America, whether through a depiction of the slave trade in *Copper Sun* (2006), gang life in *Romiette and Julio* (1999), or the dangers of the KKK in the lives African Americans in the 1930s in *Stella by Starlight* (2015), the focus text of this chapter.

CRITICAL DISCUSSION

In young adult literature, Draper's *Stella by Starlight* is most accurately described as a middle-grades book. Of course, this doesn't mean older readers won't enjoy the book or that it doesn't have a place in the upper grades as a choice for self-selected reading or as part of a sophisticated text set about social justice to accompany the teaching of *To Kill a Mockingbird* or *Roll of Thunder, Hear My Cry*. Too often the powers that be worry about Lexile scores instead of focusing on literary quality (Bickmore, 2005), complex ideology (Hollindale, 1992), and readability that do far more to attract student interest.

Upon its debut, *Stella by Starlight* began receiving starred reviews from a number of publications. In the publishing world, stars are not awarded casually but often indicate the quality of the literature being reviewed. Starred reviews from *Kirkus Review*, *Publishers Weekly*, *Shelf Awareness for Readers*, and the *School Library Journal* all indicate this text as a work of quality literature with strong character development, as represented by Draper's presentation of Stella and Jojo as well as the construction of a setting that captures the reality of rural life experienced by African Americans.

Strong characters with a well-drawn setting that imbues a sense of both time and place are two of the literary elements marking *Stella by Starlight* as a work of exceptional literary quality. These elements, combined with the themes of family, memory, and loyalty, provide teachers with an abundance of opportunities to engage students in activities that allow them to see a strong African American family and a strong female character.

Creating a work of historical fiction that feels present and engaging is a remarkable achievement. By the time *Stella by Starlight* had been in the hands of readers for a year, it had received several awards, including the 2016 Charlotte Huck Award for Outstanding Fiction for Children from the National Council of Teachers of English and Kirkus Best Middle Grade Fiction Award for 2015, and been named one of *New York Times*'s Notable Children's Books of 2015. All agreed Draper's book met the challenge of literary quality.

INSTRUCTIONAL ACTIVITIES

With certain novels, such as Draper's *Stella by Starlight*, it may be necessary to engage in some whole-class discussion about the KKK, its history, and its role in suppressing voter registration and the upward mobility of African Americans in general. Of equal importance is the need to ensure the focus of instruction does not end with the trauma caused by racism. With this in mind, most of the activities included below will focus on other elements of the story.

What follows are suggestions for before-, during-, and after-reading activities to be completed by individuals, in small groups, or as a whole class. These activities will address a variety of themes and other literary elements found in the text. Such activities not only allow students to demonstrate their understanding of the text but also provide students the opportunity to engage in activities and practice mastery of a variety of standards within the English language arts curriculum.

It is also important to notice that some activities may be presented from individual work and growing in size to whole-group instruction, but the actual order of their classroom performance may depend on the needs of the students, the teachers' preference, and the instructional flow of the unit. Teachers can use the activities as templates they can modify for the particular needs of their students or apply them to a different text altogether.

Before Reading

Individual Activity

This entire novel is a remembrance of sorts. Draper channeled her family stories and built them into the creation of Stella and the town of Bumblebee. Draper's stories include encounters with the Klan, walking dirt roads into town, and attending one-room schools. Each family possesses their own version of these stories: stories of how grandparents or great-grandparents immigrated to America and tales parents share about growing up in a time that seems distant and historical.

The act of writing a story may seem daunting to students, even if they are active verbal storytellers in their own right. Draper's own words about creating this story can provide guidance. The dedication page of the novel is an excellent resource for this. While the teacher or a selected student reads aloud the dedication page, students should be asked to consider their own family histories and experiences.

Have students identify two or three family stories that could be the catalyst for a story of their own. Once students have jotted down several possible family stories, ask them to focus on a single story. These stories do not have to be transformational or enlightening, but it is important for students to realize they also have family memories that may shape who they are and how they envision the world.

Give them time to free write about why the experience or event is strong enough to be the focus of a story. Ask them to explain why they believe others would be interested in this story. Do they already have in mind a lesson to be learned or a moral of the story, or is it just a funny story? Or is it, perhaps, an important moment in their family history?

Each individual teacher can determine how in depth to go with this assignment. Depending on the instructional goals, students can create entire stories or just complete the brainstorming/prewriting portion. This activity can be done as a journal entry or a more formal writing assignment. Another option is to have students return to this activity throughout the course of the novel and add elements—can they expand the setting, can they further define the characters involved, and so on. As they see how Draper develops her story, they might be inspired to add to theirs.

Small-Group Activity

There is a lot of information available regarding what life was like during the time the story takes place. Teachers should be aware of their students' prior knowledge. This information is useful to help teachers determine what information needs to be explicitly taught or where there may be knowledge gaps.

An interesting way for teachers to assess prior knowledge is through the following small-group activity. In small groups, give students a character that appears in the story and have the groups work to explain what life would have been like for said character or someone like him or her (see textbox 7.1). Students should include their understanding of school or work and what life was like in the community as a whole (e.g., hobbies, living arrangements, encounters with other people). If these understandings are shared with the entire class, students can refer back to this activity during their reading to see how their expectations of life during this time compare to what the characters are experiencing during the story.

TEXTBOX 7.1   CHARACTERS

An African American kindergarten student
An African American middle school student
An African American high school student
A White kindergarten student
A White middle school student
A White high school student
A White parent
An African American parent
A sheriff
A White store owner
An African American teacher in a one-room schoolhouse

Whole-Class Activity

Building background is often a prereading activity. Given the content and time period of *Stella by Starlight*, there are several things that can be addressed prior to starting the novel. This activity focuses on the author's use of symbolism. In the story, Stella receives a couple of gifts she values, not just because of what they are but also because of what they symbolize. When investigating symbolism, students think about the literal meaning of words and symbols as well as the secondary, often more figurative, meaning.

Before starting the novel, teachers can provide students with a list of items that appear throughout the story (see textbox 7.2). Students should work individually to identify and record their most basic understanding of the items and then engage in a class discussion of the items and students' predictions of what the symbol might represent in the story.

TEXTBOX 7.2   POSSIBLE SYMBOLS

Typewriter	Purple bracelet
Dragons	Cigar box
Penny candy	Textbooks given to Stella's school

Students can continue to work on this as they read, adding what the item represents in the story. Students should be reminded there is no single right answer. Instead, students should focus on gaining an understanding of symbolism and how everyday items can be imbued with a deeper meaning depending on the setting or situation.

During Reading

During reading, teachers can form activities that engage students in individual, small-group, and whole-group activities. Students can explore these embedded treasures and add dimensions to characters, themes, setting, and time period and gain a great appreciation of the novel's craftsmanship.

One of the messages throughout Draper's novel is the difference an individual can make on a place, a person, or a group of people. Stella makes a difference when she saves Hazel during the house fire. She makes a difference when her mother is bitten by the snake. Stella's father, Pastor Patton, and Mr. Spencer make a difference by registering to vote. Pastor Patton discusses how nothing will improve, until something changes. These men are making their world better for themselves, their families, and their children. These men are concerned that there may be retribution, which there is; they know that voting is necessary to improve life for them and future generations.

Individual Activity

Early in the story Stella and Tony have a conversation about Eddie Tolan, a Black Olympian nicknamed "Midnight Express." He won gold medals in the 1932 Olympics. His story is particularly interesting considering the segregation and racism rampant in the United States at the time. There are plenty of other stories of Olympians who overcame obstacles either to reach the Olympics or in returning to the United States after the event. Too often when teaching a novel, teachers rush students through the work without considering there are often a host of interesting facts, ideas, allusions, and themes along the way.

Many Olympians were the first, or most notable, within a marginalized community to participate in the Olympics. Students should investigate Olympians who stand out because of their gender, race, sexual identity, orientation, religion, or ethnic identity (see textbox 7.3). The goal is to have them investigate the many ways in which national identity or social norms are supported or ignored during the Olympics. If a teacher chooses to assign this to students, there is a follow-up activity—a gallery walk—in the after-reading assignments for students to share their research with their classmates.

TEXTBOX 7.3 POSSIBLE OLYMPIANS TO RESEARCH

Lou Gehrig	Tiffany Abreu	Peter Norman
Muhammad Ali	Jessica Gallagher	Megan Rapinoe
Eric Liddell	Hayley Wickenheiser	Andrei Tanichev
Ibtihaj Muhammad	Ralph H. Metcalfe	Caster Semenya
Jesse Owens	John Carlos	

Small-Group Activity

Music has long been considered a window into a person, a community, or society as a whole. It can be used to convey feelings and emotions about a subject or to improve a person's mood. Songs can also be used as tools to foster change in individual communities or in society at large.

There is a long history of music within the African American community. Many musical genres have an origin within the Black community, but beyond that, music has been used for various purposes within the community going back to the time of slavery. Slaves used songs and spirituals to talk about escaping to the North and fleeing slavery. They encoded their songs with secret messages about routes, passages, and safe times to travel.

Stella by Starlight does not include any aspects of slavery, but Draper upholds the long-standing tradition of using songs to convey meaning and emotions. Throughout the story, Draper uses songs in three main settings: church, school, and the neighborhood. These locations are often considered the cornerstones of the African American community. In each instance the song serves a purpose far greater than just being a form of musical entertainment. In each instance there is an underlying meaning and history behind the song selection that complements the story at that point.

As students engage in the reading, they should pay special attention to the songs included in the story. Teachers can choose to have each small group work on the same song as it appears in the story or have each group work on a different song. Either way, students should focus on the lyrics and the literary devices used within the song. They should also look into how the song connects to each specific event and what it adds to the scene. Although this is listed as a small-group activity, it could work just as well as an individual or whole-class activity.

Whole-Class Activity

Teachers frequently wonder why students do not look closely at specific passages in a text, but teachers themselves seldom take the time to stop in the middle of reading a novel to ask students what part of the novel they find intriguing. This activity, called rendered reading, can be done at several points during the novel. Several recommended stopping points are at the middle, the three-quarters mark, and at the end of the novel. Rendered reading is a planned activity that asks students to come to class ready to share two to three passages—not longer than a paragraph or two—they feel are important. From those passages they also select a single sentence and a single word.

The passages can represent several ideas. It might be a passage that captures the theme of the book, reveals the emotions or feelings of a character, the description of a setting, a moment of foreshadowing, or something that clarifies the meaning of a symbol, or it might be something the student does not understand or keeps thinking about. This is especially good for students who are reluctant to read when called on without warning. Students can select their passages, snap a picture of them on their phone, transfer them to a three-by-five index card, or mark them with a sticky note in their book.

As students practice reading their passages, they can work on deciding which sentence is most important. Then they can determine which word best captures the idea, mood, or tone of the selection. To begin, a rendered reading is not an opportunity for discussion. Students will be asked to read their passage without comment, with the class's attention moving quickly from student to student.

Turn-taking can move up and down rows or around tables if students are situated in groups. To break the monotony of doing things in a predictable order, teachers could also pass out numbered cards and ask students to pay attention as they begin with number one and proceed through the number of students in the class. Teachers can ask students to state their number before reading to help students mark the class's progress. It does not matter if students have the same passage. Everyone takes their turn without commentary. Students should be asked to take note of passages and ideas that capture their attention.

After the first round, the class repeats the activity with each student reading her or his single sentence, and then again with participants reading their word. After all three rounds, the teacher begins a class discussion about which ideas emerged from the selected passages, sentences, and words. Students can discuss the themes, characters, and important moments in the plot. Discussion should also include passages students believe show the book's thematic progress or memorable moments at this point in the novel study. Classes can record their thoughts collectively on the board or within a shared Google document.

Students can make notes about passages they believe should be revisited as well as passages or sentences students might find useful as they prepare to write about characters, themes, symbols, or setting. Through the discussion, students learn that others see and remember things they missed in the novel. Teachers can enhance this activity by having students discuss in small groups as they attempt to pull together passages that focus on the same concept, thereby building a body of evidence to support claims that might be made during an oral presentation, test, or essay.

Another interesting modification of a rendered reading can be done at the halfway point of the novel or upon concluding. In this modification, the teacher divides the total number of pages covered up to that point by the number of students in the class. So, in a class of thirty students and a three-hundred-page novel, each student would be given a ten-page segment to explore and use to select their passage, sentence, and word. In this modification, students present their passages in the linear order of the storyline. This method provides a small rendered reading of the book up to the halfway point or of the full novel.

After Reading

Individual Activity

Stella spends most of the story lamenting her writing abilities but also being enamored with the art of writing. Although she does not do well on her school assignments, Stella enjoys writing about things she sees and experiences as well as her thoughts on the objects, events, and activities around her. Many students are similar to Stella. They struggle with the topics and prompts provided but like the act of writing as a mode of communication. By the end of the story, Stella finds her place as a writer, which most teachers would love to see happen in their classrooms. (Stella's stories can be found in chapters 9, 11, 16, 19, 23, 25, and 31.)

For this assignment, ask students to write about five things for each sense: five things they have seen, heard, smelled, touched, and tasted. It is up to the teacher to determine if this list should cover the course of the student's life or be focused within a particular time frame, such as during the previous week. From this list students should complete a timed write about the topic. The teacher can determine how much time to give students and any other specifications.

Small-Group Activity

A great deal of Draper's story focuses on the town of Bumblebee and the sense of community its citizens share. Throughout the novel, Draper centers the communal relationship of the characters, especially when someone is in need. Some examples are the following: the impromptu potluck Stella's mother plans for Spoon Man, the bucket brigade formed when the Klan burns down the Spencers' house, the walk through town to vote for the first time, caring for Tony after his attack, and Mama after her snakebite.

As a group, students should look at the communities they are a part of and how they compare to the ones depicted in the novel. Students should focus on the value of unity within social interaction. They will look at how the current society defines community and determines its members. In addition, in the story many different characters benefit from the "wealth" of the neighborhood. To deepen students' conversations, give each group a particular population from the neighborhoods that attend their school. Students will then look into the role/function of that group and how they give and receive help from the community.

Whole-Class Activity

Now that the novel is finished, students should have an understanding of the impact various characters had on the town of Bumblebee and their fellow citizens. One of the during-reading activities above was to have students research Olympians who broke through societal barriers and their reception in their own communities.

Once the novel and research are completed, students should compile their research into a presentation, report, or other format as outlined by the teacher. These presentations should then be shared with the class through a gallery walk in which students can walk around and review the information compiled by their peers.

If the research was not done as a during-reading activity, teachers could elect to have students complete it at this point and still culminate with the gallery walk or other sharing of the research.

Bonus Activity

If funds are available, a teacher could order several texts like the one in textbox 7.4. As we get further and further from the actual Depression era, many students are completely unfamiliar with this period. In addition, it is increasingly unlikely they will have relatives who lived through the experience with whom they might have conversations. Providing books for students to self-select or that can be used in literature circles creates additional opportunities for individual, small-group, and whole-class follow-up activities.

TEXTBOX 7.4   YOUNG ADULT NOVELS SET IN AND AROUND THE GREAT DEPRESSION

Stella by Starlight by Sharon Draper
Mississippi Trial, 1955 by Chris Crowe
Roll of Thunder, Hear My Cry by Mildred Taylor
Bud, Not Buddy by Christopher Paul Curtis
Esperanza Rising by Pam Muñoz Ryan
Out of the Dust by Karen Hesse
A Year Down Yonder by Richard Peck
Looking for Me by Betsy Rosenthal
Mississippi Bridge by Mildred D. Taylor
Stanley and Hazel by Joe Schaffer
All the Stars Denied by Guadalupe Garcia McCall

This text set includes novels with race as an issue, but the list focuses on a variety of social justice issues that lead into and flow out of the Great Depression, before the civil rights movement. Issues include segregation, immigration, migration, deportation, poverty, class struggle, and racial and ethnic identity. Teachers can include them as self-selected choices or literature-circle selections accompanying a unit on traditional choices like *To Kill a Mockingbird* or *Roll of Thunder, Hear My Cry* or a more adventurous unit focusing on less frequently used books that are equal in literary quality (Bickmore, 2005), like *Stella by Starlight* or *Bud, Not Buddy*.

CONCLUSION

Sharon Draper's *Stella by Starlight* can be used many different ways within a classroom setting. Listed above are just some of the possible activities that can be completed with students. Teachers can complete these activities in their classroom while reading this novel or use them as a model to adjust for other novels or assigned texts.

REFERENCES

Bickmore, S. T. (2005). Language at the heart of the matter: Bridging the past and the future with symbolic language and ideology in *The heart of a chief. Alan Review*, *32*(3), 12–24.

Bishop, R. S. (1990). Mirrors, windows, and sliding glass doors. *Perspectives*, *6*(3), ix–xi.

Draper, S. (1999). *Romiette and Julio*. New York: Atheneum.

Draper, S. (2006). *Copper sun*. New York: Atheneum.

Draper, S. (2015). *Stella by starlight*. New York: Atheneum.

Hollindale, P. (1992). Ideology and the children's book. In P. Hunt (Ed.), *Literature for children: Contemporary criticism* (pp. 19–40). London: Routledge.

Milken Award. Retrieved from https://www.milkeneducatorawards.org/educators/view/sharon-draper.

Chapter 8

An Examination of Who We Are through Historical Fiction

Using Christopher Paul Curtis's
The Journey of Little Charlie
as a Magnifying Glass

Shanetia P. Clark

There are few books that I describe as "perfect." This description goes to a book that has memorable characters and a plot that moves me and reaches the emotional core within me. An added bonus for a "perfect" book is one that sparks creative, critical, and challenging questions about the world—both local and global—for both me and my students. The first book that I placed the label of "perfect" on was Christopher Paul Curtis's Newbery Medal–winning title *Bud, Not Buddy* (1999). And the second is *The Journey of Little Charlie* (2018).

When I taught middle school, *Bud, Not Buddy* was on the curriculum. It was a favorite across all my classes. Certain scenes, like when Todd jams the Ticonderoga pencil in Bud's nose all the way to the "R," generated quite a buzz. Gasps of horror filled the room when my students realized *just how far* the "R" is down the pencil.

Another scene that stands out is when Bud is missing his mom and falls asleep under the Christmas tree at the library wrapped in the blanket that still smells like her. I noticed tears and chokes of sadness around the room as I read this scene aloud. There was a collective gasp then sigh of relief when Lefty Lewis and Bud were able to leave after being pulled over at night by the police officer. Curtis's vivid imagery and development of character moved my students, moved me, and moved this wonderful book into the category of "perfect."

CRITICAL RECEPTION

Christopher Paul Curtis is an award-winning author who continues to affect young people to this day. He wrote historical fiction that humanized the

77

Great Depression from the point of view of a young African American boy in Michigan. Curtis put a human face on "Hooverville" and those who waited in line for food at the shelter. He allowed readers to empathize with the magnitude and "awesomeness" of economic despair.

He looked directly at racism and the fear of and for African American men being pulled over by police when alone at night. He found moments of joy during the social upheaval and despair of the civil rights movement. Through his writing, Curtis masterfully helped young people imagine the past and make connections to today. His literary contributions that tell the stories of African Americans in the genre of historical fiction have made an indelible impression on the body of literature for young people.

In other words, Christopher Paul Curtis is a change agent within the world of young adult literature. Even though his works speak to adults and teenagers, Curtis's sweet spot trends toward the middle grades, the young end of the young adult literature spectrum. Curtis has been a fixture in the world of literature for young people since *The Watsons Go to Birmingham–1963* (1995). Although his work is mostly in historical fiction, it speaks to issues and topics that still resonate today. Teachers, young people, and scholars alike appreciate the multiple layers of his work.

Historical fiction storytelling is important for teachers and students. It enables readers to "walk in the lives" of those who lived in that time, to ask questions and imagine why certain things happened and how those happenings affect society today. Curtis does not shy away from the ugly history of the United States, and his National Book Award finalist *The Journey of Little Charlie* (2018) takes the blinders off of an aspect of slavery. Young people will question larger issues of family bonds, privilege, and the terrors of slavery. This book is a companion book to *Elijah of Buxton* (2012) and *The Madman of Piney Wood* (2014).

CRITICAL DISCUSSION

The Journey of Little Charlie tells the story of Little Charlie Bobo, the twelve-year-old son of a White sharecropper just outside of Possum Moan, South Carolina. His father, Big Charlie, was the head of the household until he died in a freak accident. Little Charlie and his mother discover that Big Charlie had debts that now need to be repaid. Cap'n Buck, the slave catcher and overseer of the neighboring farm owned by the Tanner family, calls on Little Charlie and his mother to settle Big Charlie's debts.

Prior to his death, Big Charlie had agreed to go north with Cap'n Buck and was given fifty dollars as a partial payment. When Big Charlie dies, Cap'n Buck comes to the Bobos' home seeking repayment or for another member of the family to travel north to "run us down some thieves. Ten years ago, they stole jus' about four thousand dollars from Mr. Tanner. . . . They set up in Dee-troit, Mitch-again. Ten years has gone by and they up there thinking they got 'way with it; they let themselves get careless" (Curtis, 2018, p. 63).

Cap'n Buck is a dangerous man. Little Charlie describes him as

> nothing but a scrap of a person not much taller than Ma. He always 'peared to be gigantic when he was tearing strips offen someone's back or barking orders from atop his horse or when he was getting whispered 'bout in folks' gossip. His legs was so bowed that most of his tallness was going sideways 'stead of up. . . . [His] moustache was growed so wild that it hung o'er his lips like thik Spanish moss in a swamp. (Curtis, 2018, pp. 41 and 47)

Cap'n Buck relishes the fear he ignites in the town: "I spent all these years getting these hicks and darkies to know me real good and to see real clear where the lines is drawed" (Curtis, 2018, p. 57). Big Charlie says, "That blackheart Cap'n Buck, someone who does 'em things for reasons other than duty, ain't got no soul. I won't never go back there, I don't care if we gots to eat rocks; nothing's worth having to see what I jus 'seent. Nothing" (Curtis, 2018, p. 43). Ma recalls, "But what your pa tolt me the cap'n done to chirren to get back at they ma and pa sets me shivering jus' thinking 'bout it" (Curtis, 2018, p. 52). Cap'n Buck is a force that embodies destructive power.

Even though the town fears Cap'n Buck, Little Charlie also sees the other side of his reputation: "They all say you's the sickest, most vile piece of garbage on this earth" (Curtis, 2018, p. 59). Little Charlie is able to see that beneath the veneer is an insecure and mediocre man. Cap'n Buck "smelt worst than something warm that dropped out of the south end of a sick northbound goat" (Curtis, 2018, p. 82). Little Charlie's mistrust and eventual hatred of Cap'n Buck leads him to a breakthrough in character and action that will save lives.

Curtis notes that *The Journey of Little Charlie* is different from his previous books. In it he writes from the perspective of a White character, a twelve-year-old sharecropper's son; his other books center on African American protagonists. This shift enabled Curtis to bring us, the readers, into a world in which the main character can interrogate the viciousness and inhumanity of slavery and allude to themes that are relevant today.

INSTRUCTIONAL ACTIVITIES

An Examination of History

Curtis anchors the story within *The Journey of Little Charlie* to unpack the U.S. Fugitive Slave Act of 1850. This law "forcibly compelled citizens to assist in the capture of runaways. It also denied enslaved people the right to a jury trial and increased the penalty for interfering with the rendition process to $1,000 and six months in jail" (History.com, 2020).

Furthermore, "on its face, the new law simply set out to enforce the U.S. Constitution, specifically Article IV, Section 2, Clause 3, which declared that slaves did not become free simply by escaping to a free state and thus stipulated their return to their lawful masters" (Cobb, 2015). The act allows Cap'n Buck and Little Charlie to travel to Detroit (and Canada) to capture and return the enslaved people back to South Carolina.

To begin, have students research and report on the U.S. Fugitive Slave Act of 1850. Little Charlie travels with Cap'n Buck under the auspices of this act. Cap'n Buck explains to him, "Naw, fool, they didn't steal no money, they was worth four thousand dollars when they run 'way ten years ago. They stole they own selfs" (Curtis, 2018, p. 117). This stance of stealing "they own selfs" allows Cap'n Buck to forcibly return the runaway enslaved family to the Tanner plantation. From their perspective, slave catchers, as well as citizens in general, weren't capturing and returning people but things and property.

The sheriff in Detroit provided assistance and advice to Cap'n Buck and Charlie on ways to blend in once they left the area and moved into Canada. Cap'n Buck and Charlie's mission was to capture the enslaved persons "Eloise"/Lou, her husband "Chester"/Cletus, and their son Sylvester (known as "Sylvanus"). In essence, the act protected the White people but not the enslaved. By having students research the U.S. Fugitive Act of 1850, they will gain a better grasp of what this particular act did and did not accomplish in history.

An Examination of Racism and White Privilege

Next, invite students to explore how racism and White privilege intersect. On one level, *The Journey of Little Charlie* is an examination of White privilege, and Little Charlie's actions are an example of how people with privilege can use it to support those who do not have it.

Corey Collins (2018) explains, "And white privilege is not the assumption that everything a white person has accomplished is unearned; most white people who have reached a high level of success worked extremely hard to get there. Instead, white privilege should be viewed as a built-in advantage, separate from one's level of income or effort." Little Charlie exhibits such thoughts when he arrives in Detroit and Canada.

Little Charlie expresses disbelief at Black people walking around and being able to read, essentially having better lives than him. In fact, Cap'n Buck points this out when he learns that Sylvester (Sylvanus) is living and studying in Canada: "Don't that beat all? You can't tell me that that don't make you, a free white boy in these here U-nited States of A-mur-ica, 'shamed near to death that you can't even read your own name, and this darky, who must be 'round your age, is doing Greek? That don't gall you?" (Curtis, 2018, p. 118).

Later, Little Charlie, while waiting to speak to Sylvester and trick him into traveling back with him to save his family, expresses frustration, the "gall of it all" that the Black people distrust the social order of being "less than" him as a White male:

> Much as a surprise as it was to me, I was starting to get teary-eye 'cause I was jealous of a darky! I couldn't help but think, how's this fair? How's it fair that these folk, who was right 'round my age, spent their days reading out of books and laughing and joking and whispering in each other's ears whilst all I done in Possum Moan was have my face looking at the backside of a mule or pulling weeds and working from sunrise to sunset? How's it fair that they's walking 'round in these fancy u-nee-forms with clean shoes and looking all neat whilst I was most times barefoot in rags? Ma was right, these darkies was living better than white folk. (Curtis, 2018, p. 158)

Little Charlie feels guilty after tricking Sylvester (Sylvanus) into boarding the train and heading back to the United States. He recalls another time he purposely lied to a friend and caused harm.

Little Charlie wrestles with his conscience, knowing that what he is participating in is wrong but incredulous that Black people in this part of the world appear to be of a higher social status than him. In South Carolina he was "better" than Sylvester (Sylvanus), but in Canada that notion is flipped on its head.

The book, prior to the epilogue, ends with Little Charlie freeing Lou and Cletus by removing the chains from their shoulders and getting them on a boat back to Canada. Lou tells Little Charlie, "You ain't kilt the human part of yourself off yet. And after you done spent time with Cap'n Buck, that say there's something good 'bout you" (Curtis, 2018, p. 215). This open ending suggests there is more good to come from Little Charlie and gives teachers the opportunity to introduce a common writing activity: ask students to imagine what happened to Little Charlie after the end of this story.

Ask questions about how the "human part" of Little Charlie could guide his future path. What does his path look like? In the author's note, Curtis explains:

> Here was someone who was capable of seeing the lie of what he'd been taught. Here was someone who possessed great courage to which we all could aspire. Here was someone who, when presented with a great historic injus-

tice, might have shaken his head and muttered, "Isn't that terrible?"—but instead of those words being the end of his reaction, they were the beginning, and he decided to cross a line, to step over into the ranks of the one-tenth-of-one-percent. (Curtis, 2018, p. 225)

Students can now consider the fullness of Little Charlie's character and ask, What's next? Where does his story go from there? Where do the stories of Lou, Cletus, Sylvester, and the twin girls from the epilogue go from there? Encourage students to imagine what happens and write their own stories. In his book, Curtis created characters who will forever live with readers; through this assignment, students can imagine these characters going forward.

An Examination of Voice

The Journey of Little Charlie is written in such a way that the voice of Little Charlie Bobo leaps off the page. As readers, it takes some time to become accustomed to the rhythm and cadence of his voice. Curtis wrote the voice of Little Charlie with such vivid detail that readers should hear the book read out loud to get the full effect. Invite readers to listen to the audiobook version while they follow along with the print version. This way readers gain a fuller impression of Little Charlie's character. Through this character they get an introduction to the strength of dialect, which can help them later as they encounter such writers as Zora Neale Hurston.

This book is one that should be read aloud or experienced through the audio version. Michael Crouch, the audiobook narrator, shared details about his narration of the audiobook. He recognized the book's intensity and heavy topic: "The subject matter is not light. [It's] pretty heavy, especially for a middle grade title. So that the thick dialect, plus the subject matter. It was just, it was hard. This was a hard one" (Crouch, personal communication, April 7, 2020). Listening to the audiobook version eliminates the weight of reading the text, allowing young people to focus on the narrative, character development, and other literary techniques.

Inviting students to engage with the audiobook (or as a read aloud) gives students a "special kind of access to the transformative power of story and the experience of what real reading is all about, which is to deeply understand, to think, to learn, to discuss big ideas of the world about the lives of others and about ourselves" (TEDx Talks, 2015).

As young people "read with their ears," they are able to delve more deeply into the characters, particularly Little Charlie. Michael Crouch described how he voiced Little Charlie: "[Character voices are] filtered through their personality. Because he's just, he's just naive and ignorant and he's learning and he's just making sense of things as we go along. You know, if I played him as stupid, then I guess that doesn't give him like room to grow and learn" (Crouch, personal communication, April 27, 2020). Little Charlie's character transitions from young and naïve to cynical and angry before becoming brave and bold. Engage your students in active listening while immersed in the audio version of this book.

CONCLUSION

Christopher Paul Curtis challenges readers to question the social constructs of history. In *Bud, Not Buddy*, for example, readers are asked to examine the foster care system, the economic disparity during the Great Depression, and the racial inequalities that plagued the United States at that time. *The Journey of Little Charlie* also pushes readers beyond their comfort zone and leaves us jarred.

This story, seen through the eyes of a young White boy from South Carolina, demands that readers look at the history of slavery. Curtis does not shy away from describing the techniques of brutalizing human beings who were enslaved or the way in which humans were not valued as people but as property. Little Charlie's eyes are opened to the inhumanity of the institution of slavery and the differences in social structure between the slaveholding territories and the "free" North. This book interrogates history and illuminates the remnants of that history that remain today.

SELECTED BIBLIOGRAPHY

Curtis, C. P. (1995). *The Watsons go to Birmingham—1963*. New York: Delacorte.
Curtis, C. P. (1999). *Bud, not Buddy*. New York: Yearling.
Curtis, C. P. (2004). *Bucking the sSarge*. Toronto: Laurel Leaf.
Curtis, C. P. (2005). *Mr. Chickee's funny money*. New York: Yearling.
Curtis, C. P. (2007). *Mr. Chickee's messy mission*. Toronto: Wendy Lamb Books.
Curtis, C. P. (2007). *Elijah of Buxton*. New York: Scholastic.
Curtis, C. P. (2012). *The mighty Miss Malone*. New York: Yearling.
Curtis, C. P. (2014). *The madman of Piney Woods*. New York: Scholastic.
Curtis, C. P. (2018). *The journey of Little Charlie*. New York: Scholastic.

REFERENCES

Cobb, J. C. (2015). One of American history's worst laws was passed 165 years ago. *Time*. Retrieved from https://time.com/4039140/fugitive-slace-act-165/.

Collins, C. (2018). What is white privilege, really? *Teaching Tolerance*. Retrieved from https://www.tolerance.org/magazine/fall-2018/what-is-white-privilege-really.

Curtis, C. P. (1999). *Bud, not Buddy*. New York: Random House Children's Books.

Curtis, C. P. (2018). *The journey of little Charlie*. New York: Scholastic.

History.com Editors. (2020). Fugitive slave acts. Retrieved from https://www.history .com/topics/black-history/fugitive-slave-acts.

TEDx Talks. (2015, December 29). Why we should all be reading aloud to children [Video]. YouTube. Retrieved from https://www.youtube.com/watch?time_continue =16&v=ZBuT2wdYtpM&feature=emb_logo.

Chapter 9

Finding and Accepting Oneself through Sharon G. Flake's *The Skin I'm In*

Tammy Szafranski and Steven T. Bickmore

Lately, it's hard to know where Akeelma's thoughts begin and mine end. I mean, I might be talking about how scared she is with the smallpox spreading around the ship and killing people. Then I end up the same paragraph with Akeelma saying she's scared that maybe people will always think she's ugly. But I'm really talking about myself. I'm scared people will always think I'm ugly.—*The Skin I'm In* (p. 96)

CRITICAL RECEPTION

Sharon G. Flake's debut novel, *The Skin I'm In*, while more than twenty years old, continues to exert tremendous power over readers. Winner of multiple honors, including the Coretta Scott King Best New Talent Award, the story is even more salient now than when it was first published. In the words of one anonymous reader: "This book talks about so many different issues that are still really current in today's time period . . . things like growing up, finding self-confidence, standing up for what is right, along with problems of bullying, racial profiling, and disrespecting teachers and other people that just want to help you" (Amazon.com, 2019).

Indeed, Flake is widely praised for the authenticity of her characters' voices, voices that continue to speak honestly to readers just as they did when the novel debuted. When asked about the novel's success, Flake commented, "We can't always explain why a generation would decide to take up a book, and when that happens, in a sense, the book becomes bigger than the writer. Even now, someone will tell me something about the book or their interpretation of it, and it's something I never thought of" ("The Skin I'm In Turns 20," 2018).

The novel's resounding success with young adult literature (YAL) audiences for two decades may seem like reason enough to put it into the hands of adolescents who are grappling with the issues the book tackles. Unlike other YAL books and series that focus on action and fantasy and cast important issues in unrealistic or fanciful settings, *The Skin I'm In* directly confronts dimensions and themes relevant for today's youth in a story couched in realism. Maleeka's struggles are not those of every adolescent, but adolescents who don't share her challenges of race, colorism, and economic struggle can benefit by looking through a window into her world.

CRITICAL DISCUSSION

The Skin I'm In focuses on the urban life of a young Black girl, Maleeka Madison, whose father has died and who finds herself being raised by a single mother. While Maleeka has the intelligence and talent to go to a private school, she sabotages herself due to a range of actions and circumstances, including problems with her own self-confidence, feeling emotionally responsible for her mother's well-being, and craving the acceptance of the people with whom she has grown up. Maleeka's biggest obstacle, however, is her self-consciousness concerning the darkness of her skin, for which she has been teased her whole life.

As a survival strategy, Maleeka befriends the toughest and most popular girl in school, Char (Charlese), even though doing so means sacrificing her own dignity. In exchange for completed homework assignments, Char lends Maleeka clothing and shoes that make her feel "important"—unlike the hand-sewn clothes her mother makes with "lopsided pockets [and] stitching forever unraveling" (Flake, 2019, p. 4). It's not until the school hires a new English teacher, Miss Saunders, as part of a community outreach program that Maleeka starts questioning her own choices.

Like Maleeka, Miss Saunders is teased by the students because she suffers from a skin condition that leaves her with uneven pigmentation. And in her, Maleeka finds an unsought-after ally in the fight to self-actualize and acquire an independent voice. In the end, it is Miss Saunders's creative assignments that help Maleeka find confidence by taking on the literary persona of a slave girl named Akeelma. Through Miss Saunders's unwavering persistence, Maleeka is finally able to free herself from the oppressive and destructive influence of Char and her friends.

CRITICAL LENS

In considering the reasons to use Flake's text with all students, especially those from more privileged backgrounds, it is helpful to consider YAL books not merely as texts but as "windows, mirrors, and sliding glass doors" (Bishop, 2015). By way of explanation, this concept can be viewed as a literary triptych of sorts. When Rudine Sims Bishop first posited the concept of books as "windows" in 1990, it was a new way of arguing for the importance of maintaining culturally unique aspects of literary texts. Since then, the notion that books are windows into other lives and realities has become an important trope.

But the idea of including textual narratives as windows only survives as important if the voice in the text is authentic. Bishop herself recognized this, and since her original work was published, this topic has taken on newly debated dimensions. What is meant by "authentic" now has significantly expanded, moving beyond merely capturing cultural norms or exciting sympathetic resonance in the reader. Teachers, librarians, and scholars are increasingly searching for and trying to support more "own voices" novels on their shelves and in their curricula.

In building a modern definition of "authentic voice," it is useful to examine a study of urban at-risk youths conducted by Rachel Phillips. Phillips found that the standard "classic" material given to the students in the study did little to reach them; in fact, it made them feel isolated from the world of academics. Phillips determined that this was largely because the voices in the text did not speak to them. According to one student quoted by Phillips, "Because quite frankly, many things in language arts I really don't really care about, like, I could have done without Greek mythology unless I really planned on getting on Jeopardy, so, just there's a lot of things that you don't really necessarily need in life they just say that they want to expose you to it but if you have trouble learning from that and uh, don't really enjoy learning about it, that can be quite stressful in school" (John, fifteen years old) (Phillips, 2013, p. 687).

Phillips concludes that listening to and fulfilling student requests for more relevant authorial voices in English language arts classrooms can engage students more actively with texts. This also suggests that the term *authentic* be defined as "applicable to lived experiences." Returning to Flake's work, it has undoubtedly met this parameter. *The Skin I'm In* has been in print for more than twenty years and continues to excite praise from readers (see Jason Reynolds's foreword in the 2018 edition). By extension, looking for and including authentic voices in *any* contemporary work touching young adult lives creates surrogate connections between reader and text.

To this end, Dressel (2005) notes that,

> Most readers read literature aesthetically—for the human experience reflected in it. . . . Researchers have found that readers who become personally involved in the story also obtain a higher level of understanding than students who read efferently, or primarily to recall, paraphrase, or analyze. (p. 750)

It is especially important for students who are removed from the world, but not necessarily from the emotional struggles of characters like Maleeka Madison, to read such texts as a way to create awareness of the differences in lived youth experiences.

Dressel's study focused on 123 middle-schoolers who engaged with material that, while pertaining to their age group, featured "multicultural" elements—a term Dressel rejects. But Dressel notes that, while pooling works collectively under a single category is not productive, exposing students to works outside their own lived experiences is. Quoting subsequent research by Tobin, Dressel (2005) states, "She [Tobin] encouraged teachers to arrange cultural experiences that reflect alternative perspectives in order to break down racial stereotypes, as well as to enable readers to better recognize the 'invisible' culture when they meet it in literature" (p. 752).

To further elucidate the definition of *privilege*, it is helpful to turn to an article by Depalma, in which she discusses the advantages of adopting a dialogic approach to classroom instruction in matters of race, gender, and ethnicity. Although Depalma's research focuses on her experience with preservice teachers in the English education system, her summary of the definition of *privileged students* is quite useful:

> Given the overwhelming percentage of white students in preservice teacher education programmes, courses about cultural diversity and/or multicultural education explicitly address race and ethnicity with people for whom race and ethnicity has never mattered. By virtue of belonging to majority racial and ethnic groups, white students tend to see race and ethnicity as irrelevant, and colour-blindness seems the only safe and appropriate policy. . . . Howard describes the perceived irrelevance of race as the luxury of innocence: "Like water to a fish, whiteness to me was the centerpiece to a constant and undifferentiated milieu, unnoticed in its normalcy." (Depalma, 2008, p. 768)

Sara Newell, a middle-school teacher in South Carolina who works with gifted and talented students, echoes Depalma's sentiments, even though she lives and works in a completely different setting. In exploring a unit on the civil rights movement, Newell is shocked when one of her fifth-graders asks her why segregation was considered bad. According to Newell (2017), "That student's striking question forced me to reflect on my classroom practices. I had to admit that my technique of incorporating authors of color and diverse backgrounds where I thought they 'fit' in the standard curriculum was not sufficient. My students viewed these 'additions' with interest, and could answer questions accurately about the information, but their responses lacked depth" (p. 97).

Both Newell and Depalma come to a similar conclusion. Their students lack the basic understanding of how their position, situated within the boundaries of racial and financial privilege, have shaped their attitudes about historical and cultural realities. Newell (2017) goes on to note that it is particularly important for students from privileged backgrounds to effectively engage with voices outside their own experience because "exposure to the concepts of privilege, class, race, and societal norms in a supportive, investigative, and empathetic environment can only help [my] students realize their role in our society as it is today and give them the tools and desire to make positive changes in the future" (p. 100).

To return to Bishop for moment, she also recognized that it was important for children from more advantageously situated social groups to understand the struggles of those living outside privileged social norms:

> Children from dominant social groups have always found their mirrors in books, but they, too, have suffered from the lack of availability of books about others. . . . They need books that will help them understand the multicultural nature of the world they live in . . . as well as their connections to all other humans. In this country, where racism is still one of the major unresolved social problems, books may be one of the few places where children who are socially isolated and insulated from the larger world may meet people unlike themselves. If they see only reflections of themselves, they will grow up with an exaggerated sense of their own importance and value in the world—a dangerous ethnocentrism. (Bishop, 2015, n.p.)

That said, if teachers are to consider works by authors with authentic voices to be a useful window through which students can view realities not their own, how can they understand them as mirrors that adequately reflect cultural and social realities and then invite students to walk through the sliding glass doors into the mind and experiences of someone different from themselves? In turn, how can YAL be used as an effective reflective tool for diverse groups?

Mike Cook, an English educator at Auburn University who teaches a required education course on YAL, provides an answer. He presents telling testimony about the ability of diverse young adult novels to open the minds of even his college students to alternative voices and realities: "Young adult novels are relevant and portray life as it is, which is at times uncomfortable, troubling, and unfair. These texts ask readers to see themselves in characters that are often quite different than they are themselves, whether that is with regard to gender, skin color, religious beliefs, or sexual orientation." He goes on to add, "Together, we read books and engage in conversations that make us uncomfortable and ask us to rethink our own beliefs and stances by questioning our individual truths. In essence, we analyze ourselves through books in order to question social issues in the world in which we live" (Cook, 2016, p. 19).

His general perspective is that YAL is unique in that it reveals that which binds us together and therefore invites us to recognize and analyze our differences in a way that many other forms of writing cannot. To illustrate this, a reexamination of Flake's *The Skin I'm In* shows that Maleeka undergoes a range of adolescent emotional struggles, such as awkwardness, self-consciousness, bullying, and uneven—sometimes broken—communication with her family. Maleeka's story binds readers as they share how these experiences are and are not part of their own lives.

Where and how Maleeka encounters these struggles, however, is colored by her race, her socioeconomic standing, and her gender. By viewing Maleeka through the common window of young adult emotional experiences, readers are able to reflect on the cultural mirror she provides. This is what further enables student readers, with pedagogical guidance, to walk through the sliding glass doors of vicarious experience and gain a deeper understanding of others' struggles.

INSTRUCTIONAL ACTIVITIES

So the final question thus remains: How do instructors turn these mirrors into effective doorways through which their students can proceed? Which activities might best engage students as they read and study alone, in small groups, or through whole-class instruction?

Individual Activity: Connecting to History through Role Play

"When you were little, you loved to play pretend. . . . I want you to know what it feels like to live in somebody else's skin" (Flake, 2019, p. 24).

Saunders's assignment in the text can easily be transferred into a classroom activity. Just as Maleeka begins to read about and connect with the slave girl Akeelma, students can be asked to use their imagination to connect their lives with real historical characters or fictional characters set in the past. Shortly before the publication of this chapter, Americans lost two important figures who fought for social justice throughout their lives. Both Representative John Lewis and Supreme Court Justice Ruth Bader Ginsburg were instrumental in the civil rights movement. Students could be asked to consider how they might relate to and/or emulate the actions of these two exemplars.

Teachers can ask students to connect to the past using a few basic techniques. The first is to establish a context. The most important part of any activity that involves the assumption of a historical persona is contextualized scaffolding. For a text such as *The Skin I'm In*, it may be beneficial to use the activity as part of a historical unit on the nature of slavery in American history. If a student were to take on the imagined experiences of a civil rights leader like John Lewis, they could examine the history of the civil rights movement as presented on a reliable website such as history.com. (For further resources, see textbox 9.1.)

TEXTBOX 9.1   EXPLORING SLAVE NARRATIVES ON THE WEB

The following is a list of possible websites teachers might offer students. Teachers should add to this collection.

Slave Narratives and the History of the Slave Trade
Born in Slavery: Slave Narratives from the Federal Writers' Project, 1936 to 1938
  https://www.loc.gov/collections/slave-narratives-from-the-federal-writers-project-1936-to-1938/about-this-collection/
Federal Writers Project
  http://www.savingslavehouses.org/slave-narratives-research-19/federal-writers-project/
Five Classic and Heartbreaking Narratives by Enslaved People
  https://www.thoughtco.com/classic-slave-narratives-1773984

The History of the Civil Rights Movement in the United States
Civil Rights Movement by History.com editors
  https://www.history.com/topics/black-history/civil-rights-movement
American Civil Rights Movement Britannica
  https://www.britannica.com/event/American-civil-rights-movement
Civil Rights Movement Timeline
  https://www.history.com/topics/civil-rights-movement/civil-rights-movement-timeline

The History of the Supreme Court
Supreme Court
  https://www.history.com/topics/us-government/supreme-court-facts
About the Court: History and Traditions
  https://www.supremecourt.gov/about/historyandtraditions.aspx
Meet the Female Supreme Court Justices
  https://www.thoughtco.com/history-of-women-on-the-supreme-court-3533864

If they were to imagine a similar role-play scenario with a Supreme Court justice like Ruth Bader Ginsburg, they might look at the history of the Supreme Court, specifically when women were first introduced to the court. Others might be interested in some of the seminal court arguments Ginsburg made as an attorney and her written opinions as a member of the court.

The following are two suggestions for writing assignments in which the student might take on the role of a historical persona, either real or imagined. Each has the student write in a format different from the traditional argumentative or position essay that students are frequently requested to produce in their coursework.

Journal Writing

Teachers can require students to create a series of narrative journal entries like the assignment in the novel. This is best accomplished individually; however, teachers can suggest possible scenarios for students to address. One scenario might be the arrival of a slave in America, much like the incidents that Maleeka addresses in her own writing. Another scenario might be to imagine walking alongside John Lewis into Selma, Alabama, in 1965.

Role Playing

In this activity, students choose a historical figure involved in the abolitionist movement or assume the role of a character that the student creates. Using materials from introductory material or their individual research, students can be asked to create a five- to seven-minute presentation of their character's thoughts and feelings about racial equality and slavery. Teachers may wish to provide specific questions for the students to address.

Small-Group Activity: Expanding the Scene

One of the underlying themes in *The Skin I'm In* concerns the concept of silence. Depending on the situation, silence is either portrayed as something beneficial (as when Maleeka overhears Tai and Miss Saunders's private conversation) or, more often, as something counterproductive, detrimental, and even life-threatening.

The decision of whether or not to speak up when witnessing an act of bullying, aggression, or inappropriate behavior is something that everyone faces at some point in life—not just young adults. This activity brings the importance of deciding when (and how) to speak out to the forefront of class discussion.

It also gives both students and teachers an opportunity to reflect on this complex issue—not just in the book but in daily life as well.

The first part of this lesson plan involves choosing a passage from the book in which a character or characters have the opportunity to speak up or take action. Several suggested passages appear in textbox 9.2. In this small-group activity, teachers ask students to rewrite the scene, placing themselves as a character in the narrative. Because the scene is already established, students who are reluctant writers, or who have little confidence in their abilities, may feel less intimidated by this exercise.

TEXTBOX 9.2   SELECTED PASSAGES FROM *THE SKIN I'M IN*

1. "What does your face say to the world?" is written on the blackboard. I laugh, only it comes out like a sneeze through my nose. . . . "Maleeka's face says she needs to stay out of the sun," Larry Baker says, covering his face with a book. (p. 16)
2. "The class gets so quiet, it's scary. . . . Shut up, I'm thinking. Just shut up." (p. 73)
3. It ain't no real choice when you think about it. . . . So I go in there, ready to have a good time." (p. 99)
4. (Not a specific passage, but the overall incident) Do you participate in the room burning?
5. They're after John-John. . . . I'm standing there shaking my hands and my arms like I'm fanning myself dry. (pp. 153–154)
6. The boy with the biker pants says if I just kiss him, he'll leave me be. (pp. 92–93)
7. JuJu will kick Char's butt good. That's another reason I can't tell. (p. 166)

In writing themselves into the scene as characters, students need to decide how that character would act if faced with the circumstance in the narrative. Teachers should direct students to answer honestly in deciding how they would behave if the situation were actually occurring. Be sure to note that there is no right or wrong answer and that students can extend the scene in either direction by imagining what might come before or after.

The student group should both write their extended role play of a scene and practice reading through it together. This exercise should be followed by some written responses that have the students analyze what they have produced. There are many ways to do this, but several questions are suggested in textbox 9.3.

TEXTBOX 9.3   SUGGESTED WRITING
PROMPTS FOR STUDENT SCENES

1. How did your characters act, and why?
2. If your character did not confront the other characters directly, who did they tell, if anyone?
3. If your character did not say or do anything, why did he or she choose not to? (Be specific.)
4. If you were faced with this situation or one like it in real life, would you react the same way your character did? Why or why not?
5. Do you think your character's actions would change the narrative outcomes in any way? And if so, how?

Alternatively, teachers may wish to allow each group to act out the scene that they have rewritten and then ask students to pursue some of these questions in a journal after each performance. If this method is followed, students could also be asked to do a compare-and-contrast activity that would evaluate the choice made in one scenario versus another.

This activity can be followed by a small research project in which students, either as a class or individually, investigate someone either historical or contemporary who has chosen to speak up and confront racism, bullying, or another social/cultural problem. In a discussion or using individual presentations, students can speak about how the actions of these individuals changed history and society and what the impact and outcome of their actions were (or are).

Whole-Class Activity: The Voices of Slavery

The Freedom Writers Project, as referenced in textbox 9.1, offers an abundance of firsthand stories that introduce students to the real horrors of slavery. This information can be shocking, and students might benefit from an introductory lecture. Knowing their students, teachers can scaffold an introduction using information from the previously cited websites. Information from the project includes transcribed interviews and a variety of photographs taken at the time of the interviews and from photographic evidence from the time of slavery and shortly afterward.

Teachers might introduce the information in several ways. One way would be to prepare a slideshow or PowerPoint presentation using the available images that have been archived by the Library of Congress. Such a presentation might not only show the reality of those enslaved people who told their stories but might also offer an opportunity to compare and contrast images of people who marched for civil rights in the 1960s to those who marched during the protests of 2020. Which concerns are the same and which are different?

A second presentation might focus on the teacher introducing a slave narrative. The teacher could prepare several prelistening questions, and the class would listen to a recording of the narrative. Students can take notes and at the end of the narrative be asked to share their answers to the preassigned questions. To extend the activity further after listening, students should record their personal reactions to the story and discuss the sound of the voice and its distinctive dialect and whether or not they think remembering and learning about these stories is important to the descendants of enslaved people.

CONCLUSION

The legacy of slavery still hovers over the lives of Black Americans and is evident in the works discussed in this text, in protest marches in the 1960s, in the breakfast programs of the Black Panthers, and in the actions of Black Lives Matter activists. The legacy of colorism that plays out in Maleeka's self-image can be traced to the practice that slaveholders had of moving lighter-colored enslaved people to work in the house, where they had close contact with the White slave owners and their families. Darker enslaved people more frequently remained in the fields. This created a hierarchy of position the roots of which still produce divisions.

Teachers can apply the activities presented here to books and authors highlighted throughout the text. In addition, we recommend many of the other books written by these authors. In the first volume of this series, *On the Shoulders of Giants*, Bickmore discusses the nonfiction work of Julius Lester (Bickmore & Clark, 2019), specifically *To Be a Slave*, the first nonfiction presentation of slave narratives for adolescent readers. Bickmore lays out a variety of activities that could also be added to a unit focused on a full exploration of Flake's *The Skin I'm In*.

SELECTED BIBLIOGRAPHY

Flake, S. G. (2001). *Money hungry*. New York: Jump at the Sun/Hyperion Books for Children.
Flake, S. G. (2003). *Begging for change*. New York: Jump at the Sun/Hyperion Books for Children.

Flake, S, G, (2004), *Who am I without him? Short stories about girls and the boys in their lives.* New York: Jump at the Sun/Hyperion Books for Children.

Flake, S. G. (2004). *Bang!* New York: Jump at the Sun/Hyperion Books for Children.

Flake, S. G. (2007). *The broken bike boy and the queen of 33rd Street.* Illus. by Colin Bootman. New York: Jump at the Sun/Hyperion Books for Children.

Flake, S. G. (2010). *You don't even know me: Stories and poems about boys.* New York: Jump at the Sun/Hyperion Books for Children.

Flake, S. G. (2012). *Pinned.* New York: Scholastic.

Flake, S. G. (2014). *Unstoppable Octobia May.* New York: Scholastic.

Flake, S. G. (2016). *You are not a cat!* Honesdale, PA: Boyds Mills Press.

OTHER PUBLICATIONS (AS PER FLAKE'S WEBSITE)

Rush Hour: A Journal of Contemporary Voices, Volume 4 (Paper Words)
Pick Up Game (Candlewick Press, 2011)

REFERENCES

Bickmore, S. T. (2019). Julius Lester: Author, poet, teacher and activist. In S. T. Bickmore & S. Clark (Eds.), *African American authors of young adult literature: A three volume series.* Volume 1: *On the shoulders of giants* (pp. 111–120). Lanham, MD: Rowman & Littlefield.

Bickmore, S. T., & Clark, S. (Eds.). (2019). *African American authors of young adult literature: A three volume series*, Volume 1. *On the shoulders of giants.* Lanham, MD: Rowman & Littlefield.

Bishop, R. S. (2015, December 3). Reflective paper: Mirrors, windows, and sliding glass doors. Retrieved from https://fall15worldlitforchildren.wordpress.com/mirrors-windows-sliding-glass-doors/.

Cook, M. (2016). Using young adult literature to question stereotypes, society, and self. *Multicultural Education, 24*(1), 19–24.

Depalma, R. (2008). "The voice of every Black person"? Bringing authentic minority voices into the multicultural dialogue. *Teaching and Teacher Education, 24*(3), 767–778.

Dressel, J. H. (2005). Personal response and social responsibility: Responses of middle school students to multicultural literature. *Reading Teacher, 58*(8), 750–764.

Flake, S. (2019). *The skin I'm in.* New York: Hyperion.

Newell, S. (2017). Check your privilege. *Gifted Child Today, 40*(2), 96–102.

Phillips, R. (2013). Toward authentic student-centered practices: Voices of alternative school students. *Education and Urban Society, 45*(6), 668–699.

The Skin I'm In Turns 20. (2018). In *Booklist, 115*, 55. American Library Association/Booklist Publications. Retrieved from Academic Search Premier.

Chapter 10

Narrating the Extraordinary Everydayness of Black Adolescents through the Works of Rita Williams-Garcia

Roberta Price Gardner

In her 2014 Coretta Scott King Award acceptance speech for *P.S. Be Eleven* (2013), Rita Williams-Garcia asserted, "Peter Garcia; his late mother, Elaine; and I have raised feminist daughters. We have a saying in the Garcia house: 'Our daughters are our daughters; our daughters are our sons.'" In articulating this stance, she doesn't simplify the complex and contrary aspects of being a feminist or the processes and practices related to becoming a Black feminist.

Within the stories she conjures of Black girlhood, families, and community, desire, aspiration, and subversive and explicit acts of activism coexist to resist racism within the context of everyday Black life. Her combination of cultural authenticity, unapologetic veracity, and social imagination is one of the many reasons she is part of the "new generation" of exemplary African American writers (Bishop, 2007).

CRITICAL RECEPTION

At the beginning of her career, Williams-Garcia self-promoted her books to public librarians, shifting quickly from "Rita Williams-Garcia who?" (Williams-Garcia, 2011) to an award-winning literary icon who has made a lasting contribution to the field of young adult literature. In 2009, she was nominated for a National Book Award for *Jumped*, a novella that explores a day in the life of three Black adolescent girls as they navigate the social, emotional, and hormonal tightropes within an urban high school.

Williams-Garcia was named a National Book Award finalist again in 2010 for *One Crazy Summer* (which also won the Scott O'Dell Award for Historical Fiction) and in 2017 for *Clayton Byrd Has Gone Underground*. Other awards include the prestigious Newbery (2011) and three Coretta Scott King Author Awards—for *One Crazy Summer* (2011), *P. S. Be Eleven* (2014), and *Gone Crazy in Alabama* (2016). These accolades acknowledge the significance of her writing to enlarge critical perspectives, help young readers feel affirmed, and improve social and cultural understanding.

With the exception of Clayton Byrd, the protagonists in her books are typically young Black girls navigating intersecting forms of inequality (e.g., race, gender, class, place) within the context of their everyday lives. Because of the strong females reflected in her narratives (tangled paths and all), this chapter uses the lens of Black girlhood cartographies (Butler, 2018) and social theory. These theories address some of the intertextual themes found in Williams-Garcia's larger body of work and in *One Crazy Summer*, the "tween" novel serving as the central book for pedagogical expansion in this chapter.

Butler (2018, p. 33) defines Black girl cartographers as "researchers, scholars, advocates, and individuals who self-identify as a 'Black Girl' and who have a deep concern for Black girls' health, lives, well-being and ways of being." Her theory emphasizes geopolitical and social geographies, showing how Black girls negotiate, create, live, reclaim, and adapt spaces. This theory merges reflective practice with action-oriented research and teaching as reflected in stories exploring Black girlhood, such as *Like Sisters on the Homefront* (1995), *No Laughter Here* (2003), and *Every Time a Rainbow Dies* (2001). Williams-Garcia fully exemplifies this role.

The character dynamics and experiences in her stories reveal the interwoven complexities of how "Black [and gendered] matters are [always also] spatial matters" (McKittrick, 2006, p. xiv). Whether she's addressing diasporic influences of African American identity, love, loss, self-esteem, religion, or teenage motherhood, her stories depict the ways social locations influence her characters' lives and shape meaning within the stories. Williams-Garcia ensures the social geographies never eclipse the humanity of her characters or fully dictate their being.

In her debut young adult novel, *Blue Tights* (1988), she introduces readers to Joyce Collins, a young Black girl who finds and loses herself through dance. Joyce is not yet "at home" in her own body. Although she "hides from mirrors" and constantly gazes downward, she desperately wants to be seen.

Ultimately, she overcomes the forces attempting to limit her aspirations to engage in dance as a form of self-empowerment and expression. Intersecting themes of self-love, perseverance, objectification, sexual versus emotional love, and obfuscating the predatory gaze and desire of older males demonstrate Williams-Garcia's early commitment to addressing the politics of Black female bodies, beauty aesthetics, and the desire for creative spaces to resist limited and imposed forms of embodiment.

INSPIRING "BOOK ACTIVISM AT ITS BEST"

Although young adult literature has increasingly pushed boundaries, broadening dialogues around sensitive subjects, Williams-Garcia's books have consistently gone a step further. While centering the perspectives, knowledge, and practices of Black females is inherently a radical act given the scarcity of these voices and experiences in literary spaces, Williams-Garcia's willingness to expose intracultural conflicts (Martin, 2011) and inject taboo stories and antiheros into the "hope circuit" of young adult literature is significant.

In *Every Time a Rainbow Dies* (2009), she explores life after sexual assault from the perspective of a survivor and the young man who disrupts the assault. They eventually develop an intimate relationship. In *No Laughter Here* (2003), she sheds light on the invisible scars associated with female circumcision. Both books demonstrate the radical inclusivity of Williams-Garcia's narratives and her refusal to restrict, erase, or allow silence to serve as solution to uncomfortable realities.

Williams-Garcia writes about the difficulties of Black girls living uncoddled lives without being dire. She asserts that she knew *No Laughter Here* would cause discomfort but "bank[ed] on girl activism" to carry the book. During an invited school visit, however, a group of mostly males fueled the conversation, sharing questions and concerns in a poignant demonstration of "book activism" (Williams-Garcia, 2016).

Williams-Garcia's protagonists are consistently represented as agents of strength carving paths of liberation guided by sources of communal and/or inner strength (Hinton-Johnson, 2003; Roundtree, 2008). Her stories reflect the unapologetic tone of the thirteen-year-old mother she met at a book signing "who did not blink" as she held her baby on her hip and affirmed her status as a mother (Cole, 2008). She reveals the range of Black girlhood experiences and associated layers of complexity, strength, and frailty individually and within Black families and communities.

Her characters live full lives, at times exuding wit and humor to take ownership and resist confining spaces. As Dominique the feisty athletic provocateur in *Jumped* proclaimed, "I like gym. I don't cut gym. I don't have a problem with gym. Just folk dancing. I'll sit out if we're folk dancing. Big cramps if we're doing do-si-do'ing" (Williams-Garcia, 2009, p. 93).

The rhythm and aural quality of the dialogue and her ability to capture the calm and vibrancy that coexists in working-class communities reflects a nuanced understanding of place and personhood. In all her books, Rita Williams-Garcia crafts the phenomenal complexities and the extraordinary everydayness of Black adolescents navigating young adulthood in a hyper-racialized, -classed, and -gendered society.

ONE CRAZY SUMMER

In *One Crazy Summer*, Williams-Garcia introduces readers to Delphine, Vonetta, and Fern, three sisters who visit Oakland, California, to reunite with their estranged mother. The story takes place in 1968, in the heart of Oakland, the city where the Black Panthers were formed. Williams-Garcia brings the social politics of Black childhood to bear during this time using the context of everyday life.

Delphine, the narrator and central character, is a tween from Brooklyn, New York. She is the oldest of three girls being raised by a single father (Pa) and their grandmother (Big Ma). Their mother (Cecile/Nzila) is a poet who aligns herself with the Panthers (she occasionally uses her printing press to create posters and poetry for the group). She left the girls behind in Brooklyn when they were babies. Only Delphine has traces of her in her memory.

One central tension in the story relates to Cecile's unwillingness to yield to conventional expectations of motherhood. Her dismissive behavior toward her young daughters, clothing style, and material culture (or lack thereof; for example, they eat dinner on a paper tablecloth on the floor) causes her daughters to label her "crazy." Readers are left to decide for themselves if the young girls' contentions are correct. The narrative is deceptively simple in part because Williams-Garcia writes this "history from below" (in the world of everyday people), using humor and the gaze of preadolescence. Despite its seeming simplicity, this book speaks to everyone.

Great Migrations: Race, Space, Place, and Voice in *One Crazy Summer*

The references, themes, and subjects (communal activism and resistance, racial consciousness, civic progress and participation) make this an excellent "gateway book"[1] for teachers to use with middle grade and high school readers. As Martin (2011, p. 22) asserts, Williams-Garcia thrusts readers into this "historically-situated Black universe . . . and expects them to keep up."

The settings throughout are not arbitrary, and they signify broad strokes of social, political, and geographical meaning within the African American community. For example, just as Oakland, Brooklyn, and Alabama shape the lives of the Gaither sisters and their extended family, they also represent important sites of cultural kinship, history, collective struggle, and liberation within the African American community.

After Delphine, Vonetta, and Fern endure "Cassius-Clay clouds on the airplane . . . bumping over Detroit, Chicago and Denver" (Williams-Garcia, 2010, pp. 1–2), they arrive in Oakland, where they must find their own way both literally and metaphorically. Delphine leads, and the younger girls occasionally follow. They encounter the fetishizing behavior of a White woman at the airport, who Delphine asserts "stood before us clapping her hands like we were on display at the Bronx Zoo" (Williams-Garcia, 2010, p. 15).

As the fat White woman who "warbled like an opera singer" jiggled and laughed, she pinched the girls' cheeks and pressed money into their hands (Williams-Garcia, 2010, pp. 16–17). Delphine refuses the coins the lady gives them because they are "so well behaved"; however, Vonetta and Fern clutch the money with plans to purchase penny candy. It is one of the many examples of Williams-Garcia's use of levity to mediate the discomforting phenomenon of the White gaze. Readers are reminded that Black children must learn how to respond to it in ways that won't cause them too much harm.

Williams-Garcia's decision to portray the Black Panthers using a youthful gaze draws from her own childhood encounters witnessing the Black Panthers' antihunger and sustenance programs. In her 2011 Coretta Scott King Award acceptance speech, Garcia-Williams asserted that the supportive services the Panthers provided in her neighborhood were excluded from media representations. She tells the other half of the story through Delphine's eyes. After Delphine attends the free breakfast program for the first time, she says, "I thought Black Panthers would only look out for black people, but there were two Mexicans, a little white boy, and a boy who looked both black and Chinese. Everyone else was black. I'd never seen the Black Panthers making breakfast on the news. But then, beating eggs never makes the evening news" (Williams-Garcia, 2010, p. 63).

At the People's Center, the girls' level of Black consciousness and Delphine's awareness of gendered injustice is also elevated. As they enter the People's Center, Delphine notices pictures of "George Washington, Abraham Lincoln, and President Johnson, next to a picture of Huey Newton with a rifle by his side" (Williams-Garcia, 2010, p. 69). However, she admits that she doesn't recognize any of the women pictured on the wall. In another instance, as Delphine recalls the civics videos shown in first grade, and the limited professional roles suggested to females, she says, "The film's narrator reminded every boy—from Ellis Carter to the James, the Anthonys, and every other pants wearer—that they too could be guardians of our community. We girls were reminded that we could look forward to becoming teachers, nurses, wives, and mothers. Poets were never mentioned" (Williams-Garcia, 2010, p. 121).

No, Ma'am . . . Exceptions and Omissions

Williams-Garcia also demonstrates that words matter across place and time. At different points both Delphine and Cecile resist the word *ma'am* on the basis that it's a dialogical relic of the old South. Delphine resists Big Ma's instructions on "how to talk to white people," asserting she's only heard the word *ma'am* used in Alabama and by Big Ma. She states, "That old word was perfectly fine for Big Ma. It just wasn't perfectly fine for me" (Williams-Garcia, 2010, p. 16).

Williams-Garcia also eases racial tension through the omission of words. In the chapter on civic pride, Delphine narrates her family's encounter with a southern policeman as they drive to Alabama in the Wildcat (the affectionate name given to Pa's car). They are unable to stop for food or lodging due to Jim Crow laws, so they resort to sleeping in the car. She describes waking up to "balls of flashlight ghost and a policeman who . . . hadn't offered directions, or called Papa 'Mr. Gaither, sir' or 'citizen' like the helpful police officer in the civic-pride films [from grade school]." She says, "I heard what the state policeman called Papa. I heard it all right" (Williams-Garcia, 2010, p. 124). Williams-Garcia, however, never allows Delphine to say what her father was called; readers are only left to infer. This is one of many examples of how this book's narrative offers opportunities for curriculum extensions for older readers (e.g., explorations into Jim Crow laws, history of policing people of color in America, communal responses to police brutality).

In their textual analysis of *One Crazy Summer*, Howard and Ryan (2017) trace enactments of Delphine's agency. They emphasize her liminality in various contexts (e.g., her in-between status as a girl and teen). They argue the tween perspective of the book fills an important niche because tween standpoints remain scarce. In her sociohistorical study of the literary tradition of Black women writers, Hinton-Johnson (2003) finds that Williams-Garcia's books contribute to a long tradition of Black feminist writers whereby Black girls strive to find their own voices.

Indeed, Delphine, Vonetta, and Fern shift their ways of knowing and being Black girls across time and space, finding their voices in various ways, including through reciting Cecile's poetry at the rally in Defremery Park. Nothing and no one is the same after Oakland. Even Miss Patty Cake is transformed with a black marker after Vonetta grows tired of taunts that her white doll represents "self-hatred." Throughout, neither the characters nor readers are allowed to feel at ease or indifferent to the events that transpire. As Martin (2011, p. 24) asserts, "It is prickly and uncomfortable . . . as readers close the book exhausted and pull the thorns out of their flesh, we intuit that Williams-Garcia has taken us into spaces where few authors dare to tread." Although *One Crazy Summer* is set in the past, it speaks to the present with echoes into the future, a hallmark of her work.

As this chapter is being written, the Black Lives Matter movement[2] inspired by Alicia Garza is engaging youth in resistance to the killing of unarmed Black males and females at the hands of police. Williams-Garcia's books serve as critical tools for all students to better understand how race and gender affect our lives across place, space, and time. This book and its message adds to the important role of youths in civic processes to achieve justice and evoke change.

CLASSROOM ACTIVITIES OR INSTRUCTIONAL FOCUS

One Crazy Summer includes numerous opportunities for classroom expansion (e.g., Common Core State Standards for English Language Arts and English Language Arts Literacy in History and Social Studies). Williams-Garcia's approach to "history from below" provides an accessible entry point for students to analyze history using primary sources and engage in an inquiry-based approach using the book and informational texts to understand structural racism, including how racism and inequality occur within multiple interrelated social and political contexts (e.g., neighborhoods, schools, government).

Historical fiction addressing social inequities can enrich students' knowledge about the institutional, communal, interpersonal, familial, and individual effects of structural racism. However, as readers make these (dis)connections, they may express sentiments of anger, shame, and grief or a host of other feelings (Brooks & Hampton, 2005).

The group and individual extensions below provide an opportunity for students to express their thoughts and develop logical arguments through collaborative and independent analytic processes as they cite textual evidence and connect to personal and social phenomena using primary resources while engaging in multiple levels of strategic and extended thinking (Webb et al., 2005).

Whole-Class Instruction

In a whole-group setting, the teacher will introduce students to structures of social analysis, including macro, meso, and micro structures. Teachers should create an anchor chart or a visual concept map of the three analytical levels. As the teacher defines each level, he or she will provide students with examples within each domain that demonstrate the interconnected dimensions of the social spheres.

Macro-level social dimensions include large institutional structures (e.g., national economies and legal systems) and civil liberties (a key concept explored within *One Crazy Summer*). This is the broadest category of social system.

Meso-level elements are related to specific groups, communities, and local social systems (e.g., the formation of social patterns and cultural networks developed in response to macro-level forces). In the book, the People's Center is an example of a meso-level system and was a central site where the Black Panthers created programs to support community members disenfranchised by a host of political and legal arrangements.

Micro-level structural analysis looks at the lowest level of social interaction, including personal everyday social interactions (e.g., how individuals engage in particular behaviors and conversations with each other in response to interconnected macro- and meso-level factors). For example, when the sisters watch television, they engage in "colored counting," a game in which they count the number of colored people they see on television shows and commercials. They also count the number of words the colored people on these shows get to say. This micro-level enactment is intertwined with macro- and meso-level social processes.

Small-Group Instruction

After being introduced to the three analytical levels of social analysis (including examples from the text), students can work in small groups to identify contextualizing quotes and events from *One Crazy Summer* to engage in social analysis to categorize these elements while assessing how they reflect macro-, meso-, micro-level social processes. They will create their own three-column chart with the respective social levels as column headings. Alternatively, the teacher can provide a three-column graphic organizer template.

Students will discuss why they categorized certain quotes and events in a particular column and include page numbers for quick reference and assessment. Teachers should encourage students to share examples with the whole group as a formative assessment, noting points of convergence and divergence as students categorize particular events and quotes.

Individual Instruction

One Crazy Summer includes numerous references to Black iconography, colloquialisms of the era (e.g., "power to the people"), geographical sites (e.g., De Fremery Park in Oakland), contextual historical references (e.g., penny candy), and individuals typically omitted from history (e.g., Huey Newton). Individually, students will select one topic on which to conduct an academic investigation using primary sources. Students will produce a one-page written response to expand understanding of their selected historical element in relationship to the time and place of the story. The completed one-pager should include visual and graphic elements (photos, drawings, etc.).

Since most story elements are connected to the various levels of social analysis, during writing conferences, teachers might ask students to determine the primary level of analysis. For example, a student may select songs like James Brown's anthem "Say It Loud—I'm Black and I'm Proud." This song addresses the meso- and micro-level context of racism, since it became a cultural battle cry in the Black community in response to anti-Black rhetoric and the denial of Black humanity and basic civil rights.

These literacy engagements reflect literacy as "multiple, tied to identities, historical, collaborative, intellectual, and political" (Muhammad & Haddix, 2016, p. 325). As students work collaboratively and individually, the instructional tasks unite intersecting skill sets as students synthesize, summarize, and elaborate on various elements of the book while also formulating responses to key themes and social constructs explored in the text.

CONCLUSION

Rita Williams-Garcia broadens notions of freedom, Black consciousness, gender identity, and intergenerational complexities to explore the fluid and unbroken ancestral lineage of Black identity as she narrates the extraordinary everyday lives of Black youth. Her work deserves to be included and celebrated in the canon of young adult literature.

NOTES

1. Karen Coates (2011, p. 316) describes these as books that can serve as a scaffold to "harder stuff."

2. Black Lives Matter is "an ideological and political intervention in a world where Black lives are systematically and intentionally targeted for demise. It is an affirmation of Black folks' contributions to this society, our humanity, and our resilience in the face of deadly oppression."

SELECTED BIBLIOGRAPHY

Williams-Garcia, R. (1987). *Blue tights*. New York: Dutton Books for Young Readers.
Williams-Garcia, R. (1995). *Like sisters on the homefront*. New York: Penguin.
Williams-Garcia, R. (2001). *Every time a rainbow dies*. New York: Quill Tree Books.
Williams-Garcia, R. (2004). *No laughter here*. New York: Quill Tree Books.
Williams-Garcia, R. (2009). *Jumped*. New York: Amistad.
Williams-Garcia, R. (2010). *One crazy summer*. New York: Quill Tree Books.
Williams-Garcia, R. (2013). *P.S. be eleven*. New York: Quill Tree Books.
Williams-Garcia, R. (2015). *Gone crazy in Alabama*. New York: Quill Tree Books.

REFERENCES

Bishop, R. S. (2007). *Free within ourselves: The development of African American children's literature*. Portsmouth, NH: Heinemann.

Brooks, W., & Hampton, G. (2005). Safe discussions rather than firsthand encounters: Adolescents examine racism through one historical fiction text. *Children's Literature in Education: An International Quarterly, 36*(1), 83–98.

Butler, T. T. (2018). Black girl cartography: Black girlhood and place-making in education research. *Review of Research in Education, 42*(1), 28–45.

Coates, K. (2011). Young adult literature: Growing up in theory. In S. A. Wolf et al. (Eds.), *Handbook of research on children's and young adult literature* (pp. 315–329). New York: Routledge.

Cole, P. (2008). *Young adult literature in the twenty-first century*. Boston: McGraw-Hill.

Hinton-Johnson, K. (2003). Expanding the power of literature: African American literary theory and young adult literature [Electronic thesis or dissertation]. Retrieved from https://etd.ohiolink.edu/.

Howard, C. M., & Ryan, C. L. (2017). Black tween girls with Black girl power: Reading models of agency in Rita Williams-Garcia's *One crazy summer*. *Language Arts, 94*(3), 170–179.

Martin, M. H. (2011). First opinion: "Y'all Keep Up." *First Opinions–Second Reactions, 4*(2), 21–24.

McKittrick, K. (2006). *Demonic grounds: Black women and the cartographies of struggle*. Minneapolis: University of Minnesota Press.

Muhammad, G. E., & Haddix, M. (2016). Centering Black girls' literacies: A review of literature on the multiple ways of knowing of Black girls. *English Education, 48*(4), 299–336.

Roundtree, W. (2008). *Just us girls: The African American young adult novel*. New York: Peter Lang.

Webb, N. L. et al. (2005). Web alignment tool. Retrieved from https://static.pdesas .org/content/documents/M1-Slide_19_DOK_Wheel_Slide.pdf.

Williams-Garcia, R. (2009). *Jumped*. New York: Amistad.

Williams-Garcia, R. (2010). *One crazy summer*. New York: Amistad.

Williams-Garcia, R. (2012). One crazy road to here: CSK Author Award acceptance. *Horn Book*. Retrieved from https://www.hbook.com/?detailStory=one-crazy-road -to-here-csk-author-award-acceptance.

Williams-Garcia, R. (2014). Rita Williams-Garcia's 2014 CSK Author Award Acceptance. *Horn Book*. Retrieved from https://www.hbook.com/?detailStory=rita -williams-garcias-2014-csk-author-award-acceptance.

Williams-Garcia, R. (2017). Between Delphine and a hard place. *Language Arts, 94*(3), 211–212.

Chapter 11

Jewell Parker Rhodes

Towers Falling, Hope Rising

Regina S. Carter, Bethany B. Mickel, and Felicia Moore

As a child, Jewell Parker Rhodes listened to her grandmother spin stories on the stoop outside their Pittsburgh home. Stories about "family . . . love, life and death and life" filled her young mind and seeped into her psyche. Stories were her lifeblood and breath. She blew "through [books] as fast as the librarians could give them to [her], buying whatever ones [she] could afford with the change [she] got for turning in pop bottles" (Jozef, 2017, n.p.).

At the tender age of eight, Rhodes penned her first book, "The Last Scream," which she read to her peers at Homewood Elementary in Manchester, Pennsylvania (Kirch, 2015). It would seem that she was well on her way to becoming an accomplished author, but in fact this was not the case.

Although Rhodes loved reading stories, her life was far from a fairy tale; it actually resembled a bumpy, rocky road. Her grandparents raised her because her mother was not always around. She lived in a three-story brick house, which might sound roomy except for the fact that it was packed with people. She dwelt in that three-story dwelling with her dad, aunt, sister, and three cousins—nine souls were squeezed into one space (Jozef, 2017).

When Rhodes entered the third grade, her mother "reappeared" and whisked her and her sister off to California. Rhodes remained in the Golden State until she became a teenager. On her sixteenth birthday, her mother "kicked her out of the family home," so she returned to Pittsburgh to live with her grandmother, who "took out a loan" to fund Rhodes's education at Carnegie Mellon University (Jozef, 2017, n.p.). Time passed, and it had been well over a decade since Rhodes wrote "The Last Scream." Despite this, her fascination with stories remained.

While pursuing her bachelor's degree at Carnegie Mellon, Rhodes had a stunning revelation—she could write books. She arrived at this pivotal juncture in her life after she encountered Gayl Jones's *Corregidora* (Jozef, 2017). Jones was an African American woman who had written a "novel [that] explored the African diaspora" (Kirch, 2015). Seeing Jones's work in print reassured Rhodes that writing books was something that could be done. That said, she was not entirely convinced that *she* could write books.

Her hesitancy stemmed from the sobering fact that while growing up she had not encountered any books that featured diverse characters. More specifically, she had not read any texts that contained "characters with her skin color" or those that reflected her own lived experiences (Kirch, 2015). Seeing Jones's novel lit a spark within Rhodes that ignited into a fire. She had to do something, and she did. After seeing Jones's work, Rhodes switched her major from dance and theater to drama criticism and went on to earn her bachelor's, master's, and doctoral degrees from Carnegie Mellon (Jozef, 2017).

CRITICAL RECEPTION

Rhodes is a renowned writer, seasoned storyteller, and empathic educator. Her books have been published in countries including Canada, China, France, Germany, Italy, Korea, Turkey, and the United Kingdom (*Ninth Ward* press kit, 2016). She has received numerous honors for her writings. Her debut young adult novel, *Ninth Ward*, was recognized as a Coretta Scott King Honor Book and as a Notable Book for a Global Society (Rhodes, n.d.).

The Black Caucus of the American Library Association's Award for Literary Excellence, National Endowment of the Arts Award in Fiction, and an American Book Award also recognized Rhodes for her literary excellence (Rhodes, n.d.). In addition to writing young adult novels, Rhodes has also written adult fiction, short stories, and several writing guides.

CRITICAL DISCUSSION

Teaching is challenging. Teaching U.S. history, well, even more so. Teachers often contend with curriculum pressures, time constraints, and limited resources. Despite this, they are compelled to provide students with accurate, unbiased accounts of historical occurrences using textbooks that are primarily written from the majority perspective. The perspectives of marginalized, minority populations are often minimized, misinterpreted, or negated entirely.

Rhodes's *Towers Falling* pushes back against persistent dominant historical perspectives by penning a text that emphasizes one key event in contemporary U.S. history—9/11—from a nuanced, inclusive perspective. Not only does she seek to share a pivotal, difficult point in our nation's history with young readers; she genuinely wants them to understand the significance of learning about the past in the present.

As readers delve into Rhodes's text, they soon discover that Dèja is reluctant to learn about 9/11. She shares, "The people in those towers are dead. It happened long ago. . . . I wasn't even born. . . . Why should I care? . . . Why should anybody care?" (Rhodes, 2016, pp. 72–73). These are pressing questions that many adolescents ponder. *Why care? Why now?* Rhodes relays part of the history of the horrific tragedy that occurred on September 11, 2001, in a realistic, approachable way in an effort to explain to readers why they should care *now*. She does so through the lives of three relatable fifth-graders from diverse backgrounds.

Meet Dèja. She is "an African American homeless girl" who struggles to make sense of her life. Her home life is seemingly in shambles, and her father has an invisible illness that stems from the events that unfolded on 9/11 (Kirch, 2018). *Towers Falling* is a story about Dèja's journey to discover how 9/11, her family, her friends, and all Americans are intimately interconnected.

Meet Sabeen. She is a "Muslim Turkish American girl" who lives in a nice home with a loving, financially secure family (Kirch, 2018). Although she appears to have it all, there are hidden stressors in Sabeen's life. Since 9/11, being Muslim and American has taken on new meaning.

Meet Ben. He is a "Jewish military kid" with Mexican ancestry and an affinity for art. He relocates to New York but misses Arizona and his father terribly. Ben struggles with his past as he begins to build a new future in a new city with his mom (Kirch, 2018).

Towers Falling is not simply a text in the traditional sense. It can also be likened to a textbook in narrative form. For instance, in addition to stories, Rhodes strategically inserts diagrams, drawings, and essays throughout the text. These curriculum materials speak volumes of Rhodes's role as an empathetic educator-author with a heart for inclusion as well as instruction.

In sum, *Towers Falling* is not simply a spellbinding story; it contains a curriculum gold mine from which teachers may extract thoughtful lessons to incorporate into their own classrooms. The following individual, small-group, and whole-class activities are based on the text and designed to provide youths with an opportunity to engage with the text and contemplate their respective place within it.

INSTRUCTIONAL ACTIVITIES

Towers Falling is a timely work that lends itself to an array of instructional activities. The activities described below are designed to encourage students to think deeply and critically about the sociopolitical-historical ramifications of 9/11 and how this tragedy has shaped and continues to shape this nation's present and future. Each activity can be used in isolation or as part of a larger unit. We encourage teachers to adapt these activities to best meet the needs of their students.

Individual Activity Part I

America and Americans

The teacher will draw on Rhodes's *Towers Falling* to encourage students to think critically and reflect deeply on what America symbolizes and what it means to be American. Please allow a total of forty-five to sixty minutes to complete the following three reflection activities. The teacher will ask students to record their responses to the prompts contained within textbox 11.1 on a sheet of paper or in a notebook. Allow ten minutes for the first activity. Students will individually respond to each prompt by writing a poem or prose or through drawings.

TEXTBOX 11.1   INDIVIDUAL REFLECTION ACTIVITY

1. When you hear the word *America*, what images, smells, sounds, and words come to mind?
2. In your opinion, what does it mean to be "American"?

Prior to having students complete this activity, the teacher will share that there are no right or wrong answers. (This is intended to be a nongraded, contemplative activity.) The teacher will explain that their writing/drawing will not be shared with the class unless the student consents to having their work shared.

Individual Activity Part II

After completing the first part of this activity, students will turn to page 180 of *Towers Falling* to start the second activity. They will begin reading the following paragraph: "Everything can be found right here. In New York City. In the US of A." They will continue reading until they arrive at page 183 and encounter the graffiti-like graphic that reads "AMERICANS." The teacher will ask students to record their responses to the questions outlined in textbox 11.2 on a sheet of paper or in a notebook.

TEXTBOX 11.2   INDIVIDUAL REFLECTION
USING TEXTUAL EVIDENCE

1. What does Ben mean when he remarks, "Everything can be found right here. In New York City. In the US of A"?
2. What images and words does Jewell Parker Rhodes use in *Towers Falling* to describe America and being American?
3. Has your opinion of what America represents and what it means to be American changed as a result of reading this passage? If yes, how? If not, why not?

Allow ten minutes for the second part of this activity. Depending on the national/global climate and current events, the teacher may have a class discussion prior to (or after) students have answered the questions outlined in textbox 11.2. Ideas about what America does and does not stand for and who is truly American have been hotly contested topics throughout history. The purpose of this activity is to help youths understand that more unites us than divides us. America is *us*. We are America.

Small-Group Activity

The Act of Unpacking

The following activities engage students in dialogue with their classmates as a means to encourage critical thinking and promote active listening. The teacher will break the students into groups of three or four and have them arrange their desks to face one another. The teacher will also circulate throughout the room during the fifty- to sixty-minute class period to answer questions, recenter discussion, and encourage deeper conversation.

In advance of the class session, the teacher should ask students to consider an item that they own that is significant to their lives. The teacher should note that the item does not need to be costly or new. Examples might include such items as a baseball from a winning game, a photograph of a family trip, a rock collected at a favorite fishing spot, or a favorite toy from when they were younger. If deemed beneficial, teachers may model this activity by bringing an item of their own that has meaning for them. Students should be instructed to either bring the item with them to class or draw a picture of it.

The class session might begin with the grouped students sharing their selected item. Guiding questions can include those outlined in textbox 11.3. Allow ten to twelve minutes for this discussion. During the student discussion,

---

TEXTBOX 11.3   GUIDED DISCUSSION FOR OBJECTS

1. Tell us about the object you brought to class.
2. Why did you select this object?
3. Does this object have any stories connected to it? Share that story. For example, a seashell might remind you of a trip you took to the beach.
4. Do you think there will ever be a time when you will no longer want this object? When might that time be?

---

the teacher should circulate throughout the room and take note of recurring themes such as the importance of the item not as a thing but as a connection to a person, time, or place.

Students may then be asked to list some of the objects within the story that were connected to Dèja, Ben, and Sabeen. Teachers should encourage students to think broadly and critically and not limit themselves to physical items. Providing students with a handout listing Dèja, Ben, and Sabeen's names along with small sticky notes to attach under each name with the object listed may aid in the brainstorming process. A nonexhaustive list of some of these objects can be found in textbox 11.4. The sticky notes are meant more as a mind-mapping/student brainstorming strategy for personal reflection. For clarification, this might be done on a piece of paper, sticky notes, or, alternatively, in an online platform. Allow 5 minutes for this collaborative brainstorming session.

TEXTBOX 11.4   OBJECTS

Dèja: home, school, her father's suitcase, the pink ribbon from her mother
Ben: cowboy boots, sketches, horse
Sabeen: family, home, colorful scarves

Next, have students discuss why each of the items they listed were important to that character. Students may be asked to briefly describe or list the significance of each item on their worksheet with the brainstorming sticky notes. During the above discussions, the teacher should circulate throughout the room and make note of key themes of discussions as these may be returned to during later, larger class discussions of the book. Allow eight to ten minutes for this component.

At this point in the class, students should be directed to refer to the chapter "The Talk" in *Towers Falling*. In this chapter, Pop reveals his connection to the events of 9/11 to Dèja. Ask a student to read aloud the following passage to the entire class:

> Pop unsnaps the suitcase locks. A red-and-blue tie.
>
> Five plastic bags. A photograph.
>
> His hands shake. He lifts the picture. "Let's start with family first."
>
> Three guys dressed in matching pants, shirts, and red-blue ties. All of them happy, their arms wrapped around each other.
>
> "Luis and Big Kelly. My coworkers, friends. Hernandez and O'Brien. And me, fifteen years ago, so young and stupid. James Barnes."
>
> "You're not stupid."
>
> Pop smiles slightly. "Maybe not. But ever since that day, I feel stupid. Helpless. Angry. These were my friends and I couldn't save them." Pop closes his eyes. His head sags. (Rhodes, 2016, pp. 206–207)

The small groups should then discuss the importance of Pop "unpacking" his suitcase through the guided questions in textbox 11.5. Allow ten to fifteen minutes for this discussion, during which the teacher should move throughout the classroom and engage with each of the groups to tease out substantive answers and encourage critical inquiry. Due to the more abstract nature of this discussion, the teacher may need to pay careful attention to conversations where students are not moving beyond the superficial meaning of "unpacking."

TEXTBOX 11.5   UNPACKING THE SUITCASE

1. Discuss what the word *unpack* means to you. Attempt to define it in your own words.
2. Consider the definitions of *unpack* from *Merriam-Webster's Dictionary*:

   a. (verb) to remove the contents of
   b. (verb) to unburden or reveal

   Discuss how Pop unpacking his suitcase relates to both of these definitions.
3. Use one sticky note for each of the physical items that Pop "unpacks" from his suitcase.
4. Discuss why he might have kept each of these items. Think about how certain objects were important to Dèja, Ben, and Sabeen. How does Pop's keeping of these objects remind him of 9/11?
5. Why was it so important for Pop to "unpack" his suitcase (consider *both* definitions) with Dèja?

At the conclusion of the allotted time period, the teacher should present the group with a paper copy of one of the objects donated to the 9/11 Memorial and Museum. The teacher may select the items by accessing collection.911memorial.org and selecting "Recovered Property." Have the students view the item and then ask a representative from each group to share their object with the class. Questions to conclude the class session may include those outlined in textbox 11.6. Allow ten to fifteen minutes for this activity.

TEXTBOX 11.6   OBJECTS LEFT BEHIND

1. Why do you think the families donated these items?
2. How can a physical object take on meaning beyond just being a thing?
3. Why do you think it is important that we continue to view these objects and learn about the events of 9/11 like Dèja, Ben, and Sabeen did?

The components of this lesson may be broken into individual pieces or used throughout a unit on *Towers Falling*, with each activity scaffolding the next. Students may also benefit from crafting their own questions to bring to the table for discussion or by writing a dialogue between two characters that might further a portion of the book that they wish to explore in more detail. Throughout each group activity, it is important for the teacher to play an active role by asking students to support their ideas and relate their takeaways to their own concept of global citizenship.

Dèja's View

The purpose of these activities is to help students understand Dèja's point of view and her experiences. The objective of the lesson is to understand how a speaker's perspective influences how she or he describes events.

The teacher will explain the narrator's or speaker's role in a story. The narrator in *Towers Falling* is Dèja, a ten-year-old girl who rarely leaves Brooklyn, New York, and has limited access to world and national news outside of her current situation. When Dèja attends Brooklyn Collective Elementary and meets new friends, her situation changes. The teacher will also explain that this story focuses mainly on Dèja's point of view.

The term point of view, or POV for shorthand, refers to who is telling a story, or who is narrating it. The narration of a story or novel can be told in three main ways: first person, second person, and third person. To determine point of view, ask, "Who is doing the talking?" If the narrator refers to him or herself as I or me, you'll know the story is being told from a *first-person point of view*. First person narrators are characters inside the story, and will provide most of the narrative. If the narrator speaks directly to the reader as "you," the story is in the *second person point of view*. This style is used more rarely in literature. If the narrator refers to all characters in the story as "he" or "she" and knows their thoughts and sees their actions even when they're alone, the story is in the *third person point of view*. (Firestone, n.d.)

The teacher will explain that Dèja is speaking in the first-person point of view, evidenced by Rhodes's use of the pronouns "I" and "me." For example, "*I* never talk with Ma and Pop . . . makes *me* mad" (Rhodes, 2016, p. 76, emphasis added). Here is another example of Dèja's point of view: "In the shelter, even when I'm awake, I sometimes keep my eyes closed. What I see makes me angry. Sad-looking people. Nice, but sad" (Rhodes, 2016, p. 3).

Dèja also narrates, "We ended up here—Avalon Family Residence. It sounds nice, but it's not. Peeling paint, cockroaches, and no water, refrigerator, or stove in our tiny rooms. We're squeezed together like rats. Five people in a room instead of one or two" (Rhodes, 2016, pp. 1–2). This sentence should give readers an image of Dèja's "home."

Our Stories

Using the quote written earlier as an example of Dèja's point of view, the students will create a visual image of Deja's home at Avalon Family Residence based on her description. Students can create an image of Deja's residence in multiple ways: 3-D art, paper, pencil, crayons, paint, computer images, diorama, etc. Each student will show and discuss his/her point of view of where Deja is living.

Whole-Group Activity

Perspectives on 9/11

There are events in history that people do not have firsthand knowledge about because they were not born at the time or were too young to remember. Teachers will lead a discussion with the class on how they feel when a group of people know about something that they do not. Teachers will give an account of what they witnessed or the emotions they felt on September 11, 2001, to the class. Dèja does not know about 9/11, but some of her peers do (Rhodes, 2016, p. 33). The students will write a paragraph or create a visual that showcases what they know about 9/11. The students will share how Dèja's knowledge about 9/11 evolves throughout the story and compare it to their own evolution.

Interviews about 9/11

Teachers can close the lesson by having students interview adults who are old enough to remember the events of 9/11. The students will list questions they would like to ask interviewees about their experiences on 9/11. They will be able to get the points of view of the people they are interviewing. After the interviews, students will present their interviews publicly in the form of a newsletter, drawings, videos, or audio recordings.

CONCLUSION

The events of September 11, 2001, took many by surprise. What occurred was unfathomable and should never have happened. Yet it did. *Towers Falling* is not solely about the destruction of buildings; it is also about the destruction of bodies and livelihoods. The emphasis in the text rests not only on the towers that fell but also on the biases, discrimination, and misinformation that Dèja, Sabeen, and Ben strive to dismantle with their peers by the novel's end. In sum, *Towers Falling* is about remembrance; the rebuilding of edifices; the reunification of families; and the restoration of livelihoods, America, and Americanness.

Toward the beginning of the novel, Dèja inquires, "Why should I care? . . . Why should anybody care?" (Rhodes, 2016, p. 73). Rhodes not only wants young readers to know our nation's difficult, complex history but also to care about it. She writes about "tough subjects," but she does so with the realization that young readers "know that [her] stories are also infused with kindness, hope, and, ultimately, it empowers them" (Kirch, 2018). It is with caring and empathy that rebuilding, healing, and rebirth begin in our hearts, take root in our minds, and are infused into America, our home.

SELECTED BIBLIOGRAPHY

Parker Rhodes, J. (2010). *Ninth Ward*. New York: Little, Brown Books for Young Readers.

Parker Rhodes, J. (2013). *Sugar*. New York: Little, Brown Books for Young Readers.

Parker Rhodes, J. (2015). *Bayou magic*. New York: Little, Brown Books for Young Readers.

Parker Rhodes, J. (2016). *Towers falling*. New York: Little, Brown Books for Young Readers.

Parker Rhodes, J. (2018). *Ghost boys*. New York: Little, Brown Books for Young Readers.

SCHOLARLY WORKS/SUGGESTED READINGS

Haas, M. E., & Waterson, R. A. (2011). The challenge of teaching 9/11: Now and in the future. *Social Studies*, *102*(4), 139–140.

Waterson, R. A., & Rickey, M. (2011). 9/11: Maintaining relevance for the classroom student. *Social Studies*, *102*(4), 167–172.

REFERENCES

Begley, S. (2016). Fifteen years after 9/11, the past is prologue. *Time, 188*(5), 58.

Common Core State Standards Initiative. (2018). English language arts standards: Reading literature grade 5–6. Retrieved from http://www.corestandards.org/ELA -Literacy/RL/5/6/.

Firestone, M. (n.d.). Point of view: Definition and examples. Retrieved from https:// study.com/academy/lesson/point-of-view-definition-examples-quiz.html.

Jozef, S. (2017). Jewell Parker Rhodes biography. Retrieved from http://jewellparker rhodes.com/children/category/uncategorized/.

Kirch, C. (2015, April 10). Jewell Parker Rhodes: Living the dream and writing for children, children's institute 2015. *Publisher's Weekly*. Retrieved from https://www.publishersweekly.com/pw/by-topic/childrens/childrens-authors /article/66207-jewell-parker-rhodes-living-the-dream-and-writing-for-children -children-s-institute-2015.html.

Kirch, C. (2018, April 10). Q&A with Jewell Parker Rhodes. *Publisher's Weekly*. Retrieved from https://www.publishersweekly.com/pw/by-topic/childrens/childrens -authors/article/76583-q-a-with-jewell-parker-rhodes.html.

McGraw-Hill Education Pre-K-12. (2013). Point of view: Introduction to reading skills. Retrieved from https://www.youtube.com/watch?v=pv8HMBouN_s.

National September 11th Memorial and Museum Collection. (n.d.). Retrieved from http://collection.911memorial.org/.

Ninth Ward. (n.d.) Retrieved from http://jewellparkerrhodes.com/children/books /ninth-ward/.

Ninth Ward press kit. (2016). Retrieved from http://jewellparkerrhodes.com/children /wp-content/uploads/2016/08/Ninth-Ward-Press-Kit.pdf.

Rhodes, J. P. (n.d.). Jewel Parker Rhodes curriculum vitae. Retrieved from https:// isearch.asu.edu/profile/51784/cv.

Rhodes, J. P. (2016). *Towers falling*. New York: Little, Brown and Company.

Silverman, E., Kennedy, S., & Hoover, K. (n.d.). Educator's guide: *Towers falling*. Retrieved from http://jewellparkerrhodes.com/children/wp-content/uploads/2016 /09/Towers-Falling-Educator-Guide.pdf.

About the Editors

Steven T. Bickmore is professor of English education at the University of Nevada, Las Vegas, and maintains a weekly academic blog on young adult literature (http://www.yawednesday.com/). He is a past editor of the *ALAN Review* (2009–2014) and a founding editor of *Study and Scrutiny: Research in Young Adult Literature*.

Shanetia P. Clark, PhD, is associate professor of literacy in the Department of Early and Elementary Education at Salisbury University in Salisbury, Maryland. Her interests include young adult and children's literature, the exploration of aesthetic experiences within reading and writing classrooms, and writing pedagogy.

About the Contributors

Kathryn Caprino is assistant professor of PK–12 new literacies at Elizabethtown College. Prior to earning her doctorate at the University of North Carolina at Chapel Hill, Dr. Caprino taught middle school and high school English in Virginia and North Carolina. Her research interests include technology integration in the literacy classroom, children's and young adult literature, English education, adolescent literacy, and the teaching of writing. She maintains a book blog and enjoys spending time with her husband and little boy.

Regina S. Carter is a librarian. Prior to working within libraries, she served as a Fulbright English Teaching Assistant in Indonesia, where she taught public secondary students English. Her research interests include the history of Black librarianship, twentieth-century Black children's literature, and storytelling. Carter earned her BA in English from the University of South Carolina, Columbia, an EdM in learning and teaching from the Harvard Graduate School of Education, and a MS in library and information science and a PhD in educational policy studies from the University of Illinois at Urbana-Champaign. She is passionate about diversity, equity, inclusion, accessibility, and excellence within library and information science.

Roberta Price Gardner is assistant professor of reading and literacy education at Kennesaw State University in the Department of Elementary and Early Childhood Education. Her research explores Black childhood literacies; African American children's literature; and the sociocultural contexts and policy implications of race, place, gender, and social class. Her work has appeared in such publications as *Urban Education, Children's Literature in Education, Journal of Children's Literature, Research in the Teaching of English*, and *Language Arts*.

Tara Anderson Gold is a doctoral candidate in education at the University of North Carolina at Chapel Hill focusing on adolescent literature and digital literacies. Her dissertation is on BookTube and how young people share their love of books through participation in digital spaces. She is also a high school media coordinator and a book blogger.

KaaVonia Hinton is a professor in and chair of the Teaching and Learning Department at Old Dominion University and the author of several books, including *Sharon M. Draper: Embracing Literacy* (2009), *Integrating Multicultural Literature in Libraries and Classrooms in Secondary Schools* (2007, with Gail K. Dickinson), and *Young Adult Literature: Exploration, Evaluation and Appreciation*, 3rd ed. (2013, with Katherine T. Bucher).

Morgan Jackson is a high school English teacher in Las Vegas, Nevada. She is a member of the National Council of Teachers of English (NCTE) and the Assembly on Literature for Adolescents of NCTE. Her current assembly commitments include serving on the Amelia E. Walden Book Award Committee and as chair of the Equity, Diversity, and Inclusion Committee. She is committed to students growing through their reading and to providing equitable representation for all students.

Bethany B. Mickel is a teaching and instructional design librarian at the University of Virginia, where she teaches information literacy sessions and scaffolds instructional materials to enable students to more confidently engage with scholarship. She holds an undergraduate degree in secondary English education, a master's of library and information science, and a master's in instructional design. Prior to her move to higher education librarianship, she designed, developed, and taught English courses for an online K–12 school in Pennsylvania. Passionate about information literacy and its connection to the world around us, she encourages students to critically engage with literature and find their own place in the scholarly conversation.

Felicia Moore earned her bachelor of arts degree in early childhood education from Coastal Carolina University. She holds a master's of education in counseling from Troy University. She has taught in early childhood education for fifteen years. In 2011, Moore represented her school as Teacher of the Year. She has completed several classes and workshops on an array of subjects, for example, reading comprehension, special education, numeracy, history, and South Carolina geography, at Clemson University, Coastal Carolina University, Lander University, the University of South Carolina, and Francis Marion University. Moore has also been involved with the

Palmetto State Teachers Association, National Educators Association, and South Carolina Education Association.

Mary Napoli is an associate professor of reading at Penn State Harrisburg, where she teaches literacy education and children's literature courses at the undergraduate and graduate levels.

Matt Skillen is the R. W. Schlosser Associate Professor of English and director of the Etown Teaching and Learning Design Studio at Elizabethtown College. He has taught seventh- and eighth-grade language arts classes at Maize South Middle School in Maize, Kansas. Skillen is an active member of the National Council of Teachers of English Middle Section, and he loves to spend time outside with his wife, Rebekah, and two kids, Wyatt and Mabel.

Tammy Szafranski has been teaching college English for more than twenty-five years. In addition, she has taught courses in gender studies and worked with English as a second language students. She is currently working on her PhD in English education at the University of Nevada, Las Vegas. She resides in Boulder City, Nevada, with her husband and parents.

Nancy D. Tolson is assistant director of the African American Studies program at the University of South Carolina. Thanks to her parents, she acquired a strong interest in Black literature and culture. As a Fulbright Fellow, Tolson spent a year as a research/lecturer in Cape Coast, Ghana, researching folklore and teaching elementary education courses at the University of Cape Coast.

Barbara A. Ward is an independent scholar focusing on children's and young adult literature after serving as a clinical associate professor of literacy at Washington State University in Pullman. She was the chair of the National Council of Teachers of English Excellence in Poetry for Children Award Committee.

CPSIA information can be obtained
at www.ICGtesting.com
Printed in the USA
LVHW030957220122
709067LV00004B/110